FORCED OUT

Dave

Merry Christmas
and a happy New Year

Best wishes

Simon

FORCED OUT

Simon Bywater

The Book Guild Ltd
Sussex, England

First published in Great Britain in 2003 by
The Book Guild Ltd
25 High Street,
Lewes, East Sussex
BN7 2LU

Typesetting in Times by
Keyboard Services, Luton, Bedfordshire

Printed in Great Britain by
Bookcraft (Bath) Ltd, Avon

A catalogue record for this book is available from
The British Library

ISBN 1 85776 629 6

CONTENTS

'Nothing ever becomes real, till it is experienced.'

John Keats

ACKNOWLEDGEMENTS

To Mel, Sophie and Kieran who have helped me and
suffered with me. I'm sorry and I love you.
My great friends Tim, Pax, Mick and Ruth.
Paul and Liz who took us away to France.
This meant a lot.
Edna in New Zealand for reading the manuscript.
Simon Barker for his work and advice.
Vanessa Carty at Addenbrookes Hospital.
Nigel and Zoe who made this book possible.
Finally all the Royal Marines and Police Officers I have
had the pleasure to work with.
God bless you all.

PROLOGUE

THE SLEEP

My eyes were closed but I kept running and running. The air bursting into my hot lungs appeared to be slowing me down but I had to keep going. Sweat was streaming from my skin and my muscles began to strain. I desperately tried to get away but kept wondering why I had no shoes on. How could I have lost them? Nobody was around but I sensed everybody looking at me.

The fear of stopping and turning around was overwhelming me. I was panicking and sensed death again. A knife in a skull, intestines and horrific wounds were driving me away from the fear I was in.

With all the chaos, I stumbled and fell to the floor. I felt no pain as the adrenaline bounced the pain away.

Lying face down on the floor I kept seeing images of his face. Thick dark blood seemed to be everywhere, on the floor around me, on my hands, across my arms and chest. How did it get there? I can't remember. I had no time to remember but had to react.

Springing to my feet I suddenly realised I was in a street where lots of stationary people seemed to be gazing at me. They didn't appear to have any characteristics and I recognised nobody. I started to cry and shout out in frustration as my heart pounded in my chest. I needed to get away from everybody. Nobody understood.

But I couldn't run. I couldn't get away. I was in a paralysed state.

Every muscle in my face was straining under the pressure but I managed to open my eyes.

A dark ceiling and a wet sensation from sweat on the bedclothes woke me. Realisation of yet another nightmare slowed my pounding heart rate.

I was still crying. What had happened to me?

1

ILLUSIONS

I had just completed my largest ever cash transaction. The large black and white television set had cost me £2.50 at the local village fête. A pretty risky decision, considering I didn't even know whether it worked or not.

But it was from this particular television set, installed in my bedroom, that I gained my first impressions of war in April of 1982.

The Falklands conflict had begun!

From the initial Argentine invasion the flickering television screen portrayed the challenges undertaken by the Royal Marines. I became transfixed by the daily news bulletins, hoping the British Forces would inflict a crushing victory over the Argentines. Watching the images, I felt an urge to join them. A weird sort of jealousy came over me as I watched 42 and 45 Commando 'yomping' towards Port Stanley.

These events, happening thousands of miles away on a little island of which I had never heard, were the main topics of conversation at my school.

It wasn't all political propaganda, though. The full realities of the war hit home when a Ministry of Defence spokesman announced that an Exocet missile had destroyed HMS *Sheffield*. TV pictures from helicopters displayed the incinerated structure of what had been a proud ship. The

3

Exocet had engulfed the vessel with a ferocious fire, taking the lives of many men. I watched, appalled, as casualties suffering from horrific burns were carried from the ships.

The war continued rapidly. Though the conflict was half a world away, the media kept us in constant touch with its progress. Across the front page of the *Sun* screamed the headline 'GOTCHA', accompanied by the picture of a sinking warship. One of our highly-prized nuclear submarines had sunk the Argentinian *Belgrano*. Arguments began as to whether the ship was inside or outside the 200-mile exclusion zone around the Falklands.

But, it seemed, no sooner had the war started than it was all over, as battle-hardened Marines yomped victoriously into Port Stanley.

In early 1983 my parents made a major life-change and moved to a small village grocer's shop in Cambridgeshire. This didn't particularly affect me, apart from changing schools, because I had already set my heart on joining the Royal Marines.

My father didn't have a military background and didn't seem to realise how strong my desire to join was. As a boy he had grown up in Bangalore, when India was going through major changes. Upon returning to England, he took up an apprenticeship in engineering and had worked in this area, until now. A military career for me couldn't have been further from his mind.

My mother was from a strong working-class family; the closest connection she had had with the military was her brothers' National Service.

School seemed to pass fairly quickly, and my ambition was fuelled by school career evenings and visits from the

Marines recruiting department. Later I learned that even the Marines had a company dedicated to recruiting, a job which attracted those in the Corps who enjoyed performing, and posing.

On 5th April 1985 I became 16 years of age. Almost immediately I visited the Royal Navy recruiting office in Luton. Although it wasn't the nearest to our house, it was closest to my dad's place of work.

Entering the centre, I was confronted by an extremely large chief petty officer 'matlo', who for some reason made me apprehensive.

He turned out to be an enthusiastic person, and made me feel very welcome. He explained what life in the Marines was all about and what they expected from people seeking to join. After this rather informal interview I made arrangements to sit the required written tests. This was the beginning of the harsh selection procedure.

During the weeks that followed I began to feel that I was not getting much support from my family. They kept saying that I wouldn't make it, because I was too selfish and not big and strong enough to cope with the lifestyle. This attitude had something to do with the popular belief that all Royal Marines were muscular males and six foot plus in height. This couldn't have been further from the truth. The majority of Marines were of average weight and height.

Perhaps I did have a lot to learn about myself and being part of a team, but most of my family didn't seem to realise how determined I was to achieve my goal. The one person who did seem to have faith in my ambition was my grandfather. Unfortunately, he never had the opportunity to see this faith justified because he died shortly before I joined. This was a poignant point in my life as it was my first experience of death.

The day for the entrance test arrived quickly.

Inside the reception area of the recruitment office, where action-packed photographs lined the walls, I noticed that I wouldn't be alone in sitting the test. There were about nine or ten other young lads standing about, obviously waiting to be called to sit the same paper.

I felt eyes immediately focusing on me as I walked in. My stomach churned eerily. Glancing around the room, I knew instantly that I had very little in common with the others. Most were wearing jeans and I probably looked somewhat out of place in my best suit. I could feel myself getting hot around the collar and beads of sweat were forming under my arms.

After this initial quick glance around, I tried not to pay any more attention to my immediate surroundings. My mind was in any event too preoccupied with going over the possible contents of the exam! I was eventually called forward into a small classroom where the chairs were set out in a typical test fashion, took my seat at the indicated table, and waited in anticipation for the papers to be placed in front of me.

The first topic was English, which had never been my strong point. For a horrible moment I had a mental block on the very first question! It felt as if this block was going to last for the whole test; however, after a few deep breaths and a quick glance at the ceiling, inspiration came flooding back and I cracked on with the rest of the exam. The remainder of the paper involved topics like maths, general knowledge and very basic engineering questions.

Eventually the papers were cleared away and we were shown a video about life in the Royal Marines, presumably while the recruiting staff used the time to mark the papers. Whilst we watched the film, they began to call us forward one by one. I received my call and was led into another small room, to be greeted by the chief petty officer and the words, 'Well done, lad, you've passed.' I didn't have much time to celebrate as he quickly followed this announcement by informing me that I now had to pass the three-day Potential Recruits Course (PRC). This was designed to put applicants through their paces, testing physical ability along with mental agility. In other words, trying to think whilst experiencing the pain barrier.

Before many weeks had passed, I was on the inter-city train bound for Lympstone Commando Centre (CTCRM) in Devon. Fortunately, I wasn't alone, as a school friend, Nick Freestone, had also been accepted to attend the same PRC.

On arrival at the centre we were met by a hard-faced corporal who, without introduction, began to call out our names from the list on his clipboard. At the conclusion of this roll call he led us to the accommodation where we were to stay, located on the far side of the camp away from the railway station.

Entering the drab-looking building, I saw a number of other lads standing around the beds in the main accommodation area. I was given a few moments to drop my bags by an empty bed, then I was told to select a pair of tatty-looking boots and denims from a large pile in the corridor. I must admit I was fairly lucky because the pair of boots I selected was only about one size too big!

Back in the room, about 20 to 30 beds had now become occupied. I waited anxiously for our next set of instructions. I felt the anticipation in the air as all these young men waited for what was to happen next. This was how Roman slaves must have felt before entering an arena to face combat-hardened gladiators.

Before I knew it, I was covered in mud, crawling around the assault course, and if I wasn't there I was running in the gym or down a typical narrow Devon country lane. Some of the tests included moving a telegraph pole in teams around the assault course and swimming lengths of the pool in various states of dress.

The PRC passed quickly, due to nearly every minute of the three days being occupied by the various tests. Not only did we experience the physical effort that would be required in Commando training but were also shown things such as the indoor shooting range, weapons museum and Corps history.

On the morning of the final day we were all paraded outside the accommodation block to await the course results. While we waited the instructors discussed who had achieved the mark for being accepted to start recruit training. Deep down, I felt fairly confident with my performance as I had given more than 100 per cent effort, but still my stomach began to tie itself in knots. I wondered what on earth I would do for a living if I failed to be accepted.

Then through the early morning mist the course sergeant appeared. Clipboard in hand and without any kind of emotion he began to shout out who had failed. My name wasn't there. Next who had failed but would be allowed to return in six months for another attempt. Again my name wasn't there. I HAD PASSED! I was relieved to the point of being exhausted.

I had been so preoccupied by the course and my own efforts I did not get much time to see or speak to Nick. However, the disappointed expression on his face said it all.

He had been recommended to return and try again in six months, an opportunity I believe he never took.

After preparing myself for the return journey, I experienced something that was very rare within the Royal Marines.

We had entrusted one of the course corporals to place our valuables in a safe for the duration of the three days. Unfortunately, when we came to leave we discovered he had done the proverbial bunk with all our money and valuables. The instructors were, needless to say, both angry and highly embarrassed. Our cash problem was soon overcome by the WO2 (warrant officer/sergeant major) but to this day I do not know whether the outstanding valuables were ever recovered or what happened to the corporal.

After this unexpected delay I happily embarked on the journey home, accompanied by my new blisters and abrasions. Once home, I eagerly related my recent achievements to my parents. This felt like an anti-climax; they didn't seem to be particularly interested in what I had done, other than saying 'well done'.

Now I recognise that this was probably because they realised how close they were to losing one of their beloved sons – at the tender age of 16.

While waiting for my joining-up date, I managed to find myself work on a local farm. The work itself was fairly strenuous, which in a way prepared me physically for what lay ahead.

My own mental attitude was now completely focused on getting into shape. I adopted a rigid daily routine involving circuit training and running over various distances in all weather conditions. Many of my friends thought I was a bit of an idiot, but I later found out that I would need all this dedication if I was going to pass recruit training.

And then one morning I was getting into my early morning routine when I discovered a large brown envelope on the doormat. It was marked in large black letters 'ON HER MAJESTY'S SERVICE'. Nervously, I began to open it. A quick glance and I saw that I was to go to CTCRM on 23rd September 1985. The letter also contained details about travel arrangements and what I would be required to take in the way of clothing.

Now I had a date! But still I kept getting the impression from my mum that though she was proud of my determination, deep down she didn't want me to join. I also had what I can only now describe as very immature feelings. At this impressionable age I felt rather special at school because I didn't know anybody else who had been accepted into the Marines, and people were always asking me about it.

I now began to get my personal kit ready. I also decided to give up my job on the farm so that I could spend more time at home. The daily training continued, with the circuits becoming harder and the runs getting longer. I was spending an hour a day on my exercise bike in the back bedroom of our house, followed by a six-mile run which included stops to carry out circuits to improve my strength and stamina. Close friends began to wonder if I was insane.

Before long the eve of the 22nd arrived. Everything I needed was ready and all I had to do was pack it into my civilian-looking suitcase. Whilst I did this I couldn't help feeling rather apprehensive; soon I would be alone and I was unsure of what to expect. I knew I was going to miss the rest of my family.

We were all close, and this came home to me when I was

in my room finishing my packing. Mum and Dad came up to see me and at first there were a few seconds of silence, which indicated to me that they were both upset. After a short pause they began to make one point clear to me – if I should fail to achieve my aim I would always have a home to return to.

The next morning began early, which wasn't particularly helpful because I had spent most of the night tossing and turning, thinking about what lay ahead. In the kitchen I discovered breakfast was ready and waiting on the table, which was unusual because Mum never had time to cook a meal in the mornings, because of opening the shop. I felt a bit strange sitting and eating with everybody. No one spoke a great deal. I said goodbye to my dad and brother Nigel, as they had to leave for their journey to work.

A short while later my mum and younger brother Richard took me to the local railway station, where I exchanged my travel warrant into a one-way second-class train ticket to Lympstone Commando Centre. On the platform I noticed that the morning rush hour had subsided, leaving the platform cold and eerie under a blanket of early morning mist. We had arrived in plenty of time, so Mum took the opportunity to produce a small Instamatic camera and proceeded to take snapshots of me. I tried very hard to give a smile but unfortunately my nerves wouldn't allow the muscles in my face to produce one! All too quickly I heard the sound of an electric current fighting its way down the railway lines. I stood up and to my horror the reality of what I was doing finally hit home – this was it!

This was now the end result of the continual trips to the recruiting office and sometimes endless self-motivated training. I now felt that I had to make my first decision on whether I was going. It wasn't a schoolboy fantasy any longer; it was here now, confronting me. Either I could back out at the first hurdle, or else simply step onto the train. My heart began to pound in my mouth, making it uncomfortably dry, as the train creaked to a halt.

I picked up my suitcase and headed for the nearest carriage doorway.

Reaching the door, I pushed my belongings into the opening and turned to kiss Mum goodbye, but by now she had been overtaken by her emotions. I quickly shook hands with Richard and climbed onto the train, joining the other passengers bound for London. Moments after this I heard the distinctive whistle from the signalman and the train began to strain and groan as it pulled away from the platform. I moved to a vacant door, where I began to wave from its open window, fighting hard to control my own tears of emotion. In seconds the morning mist seemed to engulf my mother and brother from my vision. Once they had disappeared, I momentarily paused, looking at nothing, but thinking hard about what lay ahead.

After a while I returned to my well-worn second-class seat. Now I had the chance to relax and think. It came to me fully that I now held the key to my own destiny!

The journey passed fairly quickly and before I knew it I had arrived at King's Cross Station in London. Alighting from the train, I had the expected pleasure of using the underground system, but unfortunately I had the disadvantage of carrying a large suitcase whilst wearing a jacket and tie.

On the journey I had to wrestle for my own piece of space within the claustrophobic confines of the tube train. I began to wonder whether this was the start of the selection procedure, as I found my nose pressed against a stranger's sweaty neck!

Still alive and slightly wiser from the experience of the tube, I arrived at Paddington Station, where I found myself with the next task of deciphering the train departure time-table. Happily, I soon established which train to take, from which platform and at what time. Once I had gained this information, I made my way to the platform where the Intercity 125 was waiting. As I went past the ticket collector I noticed how unconcerned he appeared to be about his work. I could have shown him a ticket from my local cinema and still got on the train. Climbing aboard, I found a place for my suitcase and took up a rear-facing window seat. I began to dwell on the fact that this was supposed to be an 'inter-city' train but stopped at places like Tiverton Parkway – some city!

The journey seemed to take longer than my original trip for the PRC; however, not before time the train's intercom announced that the train would shortly be arriving at Exeter's St David's Railway Station.

Trying not to rush, I gathered my belongings, got off the train and immediately noticed the large number of young lads on the platform. Like myself, they appeared to be worried and apprehensive and didn't seem to have a clue where they were going. I learned that I had to get the train to Exmouth, which would in turn stop at the training centre. I vaguely remembered this from my previous trip in July for the PRC. This past experience turned out to be a blessing; it probably prevented a lot of people going AWOL on their very first day.

After another short wait the small diesel train began its trip to Exmouth, taking me through the outskirts of Exeter and along the banks of the River Exe estuary. From the warm carriage the scenery looked beautiful. However, I would soon learn that it would look and feel quite different when enduring a troop mud run at low tide. As the train continued I saw the far-off images of the assault course, which was rapidly approaching. Then, without warning, the train began to slow and I immediately recognised the platform sign saying 'LYMPSTONE COMMANDO'.

2

WELCOME TO HELL

A smartly-dressed corporal stood on the platform awaiting our arrival. (We being about six or seven new recruits.) He walked proudly over to us, wearing his lovat suit and green beret. For a moment I felt myself staring at his beret, realising this would be the item I was going to work so hard for.

He spoke with a strong Merseyside accent. 'Right, my name is Corporal Green and I'm going to be your drill instructor for the next thirty weeks, so you had better get used to me.'

Once he had finished calling out our names, he led us from the platform to the accommodation block where we would be staying. The route through camp took us past a number of other accommodation areas where I noticed a large amount of wet military kit hanging out of windows to dry in the afternoon sun. After this brisk walk we were eventually shown our home for the next two weeks.

This was now the beginning of the induction phase of recruit training, and thus the block was referred to as the 'induction block'. It consisted of one large room, an ablution area for washing clothes and a personal area for showering and shaving. In the main room there were approximately 50 beds and at the base of each stood a large brown locker with a name tag, in alphabetical order, from left to right around the room.

I quickly found the small area designated for me and dumped my belongings. The corporal instructed us to get ourselves sorted out, as he was off to meet more recruits at the station. Once he had left us, people began chatting. We were now all in the same boat and it didn't take long before we started laughing and joking.

The first few days seemed to pass in a haze of being herded from storeroom to classroom like sheep. I collected various uniforms and signed for all kinds of gear. The amount of kit we were given was extensive, ranging from lock knives to magazine cases. These items quickly filled the locker space and I had little room for all my civilian clothing.

Each intake of new recruits was referred to as a 'troop' and the one I had been placed in, 296 troop, consisted of 44 lads from all walks of life, mainly under the age of 17. I was given a service number, which would be used nearly as often as my name in the coming weeks.

During the first few days we were even shown how to 'shit, shower and shave' properly. I found this somewhat amazing – they didn't appear to believe we knew how to do this. There would now be no excuses for being picked up on parade. Personal hygiene is very important amongst a large troop of men, especially when embarked on ship or on an exercise. The Corps is very proud of its reputation for being clean and smart.

Many people who read this book will know what 'attestation' means, but to those who don't it is the swearing-in process, or oath, to be faithful and bear true allegiance to the Queen and her successors. The troop had to stand and repeat this oath, ending in the powerful words 'So help me

God'. I then signed the paperwork, which bound me to a nine-year contract and the laws governing servicemen. I felt as if I was signing my life away and had to think long and hard before I did so. But, like most lads there, I didn't wish to be seen as a wimp in front of all these people. A captain then counter-signed the form and I was 'in'!

Towards the end of the first week we were introduced to the remainder of the training team, which consisted of a troop officer (lieutenant), a troop sergeant, four PW corporals (platoons weapons instructors) who were responsible for instructing the military skills, a PTI corporal who took the physical exercise training, and the drill instructor. Throughout the 30 weeks the individual instructors sometimes changed, for no real reason, which had its advantages and disadvantages for us.

The corporals quickly began to show us the basic military kit with which we had been issued, like our webbing and large packs. This, to the untrained, took some time getting used to, especially when putting it together. Ironing also became very important because some items of clothing required ironing one way and some another. It did seem to get easier with practice, though, especially when trying to get creases into my white gym shorts, as they always creased in the wrong places.

The days were very long and the time spent in bed was minimal, which immediately began to play on my mind. I wondered how I was going to ever last 30 weeks on this small amount of sleep.

During the first few days we were also issued with bright orange shoulder tabs by our drill instructor. This showed other trained staff around the camp that we had only just joined, so they were aware of why we marched around the camp like 'constipated chimpanzees'. The theory was to

17

reduce the amount of bollockings we received, but it didn't seem to make any difference whatsoever.

The orange tabs were also ignored by our drill instructor and I soon learnt to hate drill practice. Every time I went onto parade he inspected me. He seemed to find every little error on my uniform, which varied from a small piece of cotton on a button, to a tram-lined crease. This was supposed to be a good training point, as attention to detail is very important when learning about military skills. Unfortunately, being picked up on parade would normally mean extra parades, or a punishment of some kind later on in the day.

From the very first day everyone in the troop was thinking about himself. This included me. I had no real idea what was expected of me. I thought I was under the microscope and the training teams were watching my performance. I overlooked the fact that I was now part of a troop. If I were serious about making it to the end of training, I would have to help the team as much as I helped myself.

Moving around the camp, I quickly began to notice the other troops. They appeared to be so well-organised and proud of what they had achieved. The King's Squad (most senior troop in training) looked so impressive as they marched back and forth rehearsing for their passing-out parade. They were like nothing I had ever seen before and I stared in amazement. We, on the other hand, were far from perfect and it was going to be a long hard road ahead.

It was also in that first week that the troop photograph was taken. The training team joked that it would be placed on the notice board, and the faces would be crossed off as and when people dropped out of the troop.

Basic lectures on military bearing, continued, as did the various medicals and the physical exercise, but in no

18

time the end of the first week arrived, thus bringing the first exercise.

By now the troop had been divided into four sections and just prior to the exercise I felt my morale was fairly low. I was very tired from the lack of sleep and had begun to miss my home; however, I dug a little deeper and tried to overcome this state of mind.

The exercise itself was called 'First Step'. It was a very basic exercise, which involved staying out overnight for a period of 24 hours on Woodbury Common, close to Exmouth. Each section was allocated a PW corporal, and the troop sergeant oversaw everything. The exercise was designed to teach us about basic field craft, from cooking a 24-hour ration pack to sentry duty and erecting a green bivvy (basic tent). At this stage we had no weapons and all we carried was our webbing and our large packs, which contained spare clothing wrapped in clear freezer bags to keep it dry.

That night all we had to do was sleep and maintain a sentry of two men. This worked out, doing a couple of hours each throughout the night and then being ready for 08.30 hours the next morning. The sentry system seemed to work well and the hardest thing to do during the night was get out of my nice warm sleeping bag. It didn't even rain!

In the morning everyone was woken at about 07.00 hours, and because we were all new and naïve, we cooked, shaved and cleaned as if we had all the time in the world. This was a *big* mistake because before we knew it was 08.00 hours and we all began to rush about like blue-arsed flies. This caused the silence and military awareness to disappear. Most of us were still cooking at this time, and my mess tin

19

contained a concoction of rolled oats and tinned meat, which had an uncanny knack of welding itself to the side. Cleaning it was impossible as I didn't have anything like a piece of Scotch-bright, and the only water was from the one water bottle, which had been mostly used to make a lovely home-from-home large brew. Oh well, I thought, everybody was in the same state of panic to be ready on time, so if I put my dirty mess tin in the bottom of my pack, hopefully I'd get away with it!

At 08.30 hours we began to arrive at the designated spot for the field parade. Ten minutes later some members of the troop were still arriving. I rapidly learnt this was not the way to impress the instructors, who by now were screaming at the late arrivals. A lesson that we would all quickly learn was that when we were given a time to meet, we would *always* be expected to arrive five minutes early, no matter what excuse could be made.

The atmosphere was not particularly welcoming, and once the troop was all together we were instructed to lay out every piece of equipment we had, even down to our razor blades. This, of course, included my freshly baked mess tin, complete with rolled oats and meat.

I stood quietly waiting with the rest of the section, listening to the instructors verbally abusing us for having dirty boots, not shaving and dirty mess tins! The corporal slowly moved along the line and the wait for my inspection made me feel physically sick. I felt as if I was about to be strung up and executed. The only comfort I had was from the fact that I wasn't going to be the only one to be told to pick up their belongings and get on the flank of the troop.

I received the anticipated bollocking, along with an explanation of the dangers of a dirty mess tin. It was fine if you only had to eat out of it once; however, I would soon get stomach problems or food poisoning from it if forced to use it for a few days, which would make me a liability to my pals.

Out of the 44 members of the troop, 40 were moved to the flank, where we awaited our punishment.

The four lads who did not get picked up were also told to get on the flank because we were supposed to be working as a team. The punishment that followed was a sharp reminder about teamwork, professionalism and never being late again.

On the instruction of the training team, we shouldered our webbing and large packs. It felt rather weird to hear the sound of so many men putting on equipment in a silent wooded area. Then with an almighty scream the words 'Right, get into two files!' rang in my ears.

We began what was to be my first experience of a 'beasting' (Corps slang for physical punishment). We progressed as a troop down a very muddy track, then we were ordered onto our bellies and told to start crawling. The experience of crawling with a large pack on my back seemed to sap the energy from my body in seconds, with my arms and legs feeling like lead. The pain in my limbs was aggravated by the abundance of razor sharp rocks, which cut deep into my knees and elbows. We continued inch by inch, with the training team continually screaming, 'Get down!', 'Keep crawling!', 'Don't stop, you fucking bunch of wankers, we haven't even started yet!' I attempted to concentrate on what I was doing rather than listening to the abuse and the sound of my struggling colleagues. After what felt like hours I quickly glanced upwards and saw part of a large frozen pond directly in front of me. I wasn't the first to enter, owing to my position in the troop, but my turn soon came. I felt the muddy icy water penetrate the clothing I was wearing. Within seconds I felt pain as my fingers and chest tightened, and gasped desperately for air.

Once clear of the water, we were ordered back to our feet. Then we underwent a further 20 minutes' physical exercise, ranging from press-ups with kit to sprinting up and down hills and climbing onto the roof of a disused building.

At the conclusion I was wet, cold and close to tears thinking what the hell am I doing here? The troop sergeant then reminded us that there was plenty more of that to come and politely asked if anyone wanted to 'rap' (quit). My morale was at an extreme low and the thought of rapping was very tempting indeed.

The waiting transport took us back to the training centre, where we spent the remainder of the day cleaning kit. Mud had got everywhere. I was now extremely unhappy and very tired. Even on a Sunday there was no such thing as a day off at CTCRM! The temptation to quit was inviting as my mind dreamed about home, underage drinking in the local pub, and females.

Eventually I got to bed, where I began to seriously think about giving in. Somehow, though, the thought of going home to all my friends who would say, 'We knew you wouldn't make it', gave me the encouragement to stay. I would wait and see how the second week went, and maybe I would get accustomed to this new lifestyle!

The second week progressed as badly as the first, I felt as if I was on the brink of exhaustion. Every day began at about 05.30 hours and I was lucky if I got to bed before 01.30 hours. Despite this, the troop was beginning to come together and I made two close friends, Phil Fulton and Mike Stone.

Phil was from the North-east, a well-built lad and keen on weight training. His months of being unemployed prior to joining the Corps had given him time to train and build up his strength.

Mike came from East Anglia and had a keen interest in boxing. He smoked like a chimney and continually laughed about everything. A bit like myself, they didn't have any particular reason why they had joined the Marines, other than ambition.

They were excellent company and we managed to motivate each other by having a good laugh and joke when times got hard.

The physical exercise in the gym continued, with the emphasis being placed on co-ordination in team-type aerobics, such as vaulting wooden horses in a variety of ways. Being fairly small, I found the gym work quite enjoyable but the lads who fell off the vaulting horse would have strongly disagreed.

Inspections had become a familiar part of the daily routine and we even had our gym kits inspected prior to starting our exercise. The white 'Bobby Charlton'-style shorts had to be immaculate and we were expected to have a razor-sharp crease running down the front and back of each leg. The footwear we wore in the gym was referred to as 'pusser's pumps' and were identical to the cheap rubber ones I used to wear at school. Allegedly these pumps were responsible for a number of injuries to recruits as several lads suffered with problems like 'shin splits' and 'CP knee'. Fortunately I didn't suffer in this way; placing my Reebok insoles into my pumps probably helped this. Even the pumps were subjected to inspections. They had to be covered with white blanco every day. It was almost impossible to keep them clean because the run from the accommodation block to the gym normally took us through puddles, which ruined their appearance.

After the PTI's inspection we would sprint to our pre-located positions in the gym, which were marked by a coloured spot on the floor. Once we were all-stationary and stood to attention, the lesson would begin. It would be extra hard for the remainder of the troop if anyone had been picked up during the inspection. There was never any let-up in the gym. The first few minutes would be spent on aerobic routines in order to warm up and improve our co-ordination. We would then proceed to circuits that punished the upper body. The circuits were always slightly different but included press-ups, sit-ups, and various other exercises like pull-ups, rope climbing and burpees. I sometimes wondered how I ever kept going as my muscles spasmed under the exertion. The PTIs continually motivated us, especially when we were hanging upside down at the top of the indoor climbing ropes. The sessions passed reasonably quickly but there was always more to follow the next day.

A typical day at the training centre didn't exist, but revolved mainly around gym work, classroom lectures, drill and weapon training. It was during one of these sessions that I began to hate the quick change-overs.

After completing a sweaty session in the gym, we would be told to be changed and ready for drill within five minutes. This meant: strip, get wet, soap on, rinse off, dress and be immaculate for parade. Needless to say, this was almost impossible; even if I did manage a good rinse in the shower, by the time I had got dressed again I would still be sweating. Then in the resulting drill inspection somebody would get picked up for having fluff on his beret, which would result in an extra parade. This kept us constantly under pressure. There was no sympathy from the training team, as they claimed it was character-building. As a result I would be up late at night preparing as much of my uniform for the next day as I could.

Commando training was dictated by a timetable on the troop notice board, and by now the troop photo had been tactically placed next to it. A few lads had already decided to 'rap'. This was no disgrace, but it was a shock when certain individuals left because most of them seemed to be coping better than me.

As the second week drew to a close I had become very homesick, but never indicated this to anyone other than Phil and Mike. They tried to encourage me to stick at it but I had hastily made my decision to rap. I approached my drill leader that evening and told him that I wanted out. He tried to persuade me to stay but respected my decision in a very unsympathetic manner. I went to bed for a few hours, continuously thinking about my decision and whether or not it was right. However, come the morning I was in for a shock.

After being told to stand by our beds the troop sergeant entered shouting, 'Right, who else wants to leave with Bywater?'

I noticed one lad step forward. Then to my horror the sergeant told him, 'Well, you're not going anywhere now, until at least week four.'

Fuck me, I thought. Somebody had failed to mention this was written somewhere into my contract.

3

NO LOOKING BACK

We had now completed the induction phase and with this came the move to our new accommodation block, located at the far side of the camp and overlooking the river Exe and the assault course. The orange shoulder tabs were taken from us and I had the pleasure of knowing that, whether I liked it or not, I had another two weeks to bear if I stood by my decision to quit.

As in all large establishments, rumours around the camp were rife. Each forthcoming exercise was always believed to be harder than the previous one. These rumours were generally fuelled by the recruit troops further on in their training who had already completed these exercises. One particular exercise, called, 'Twosome', was commonly referred to by the recruits as 'Gruesome Twosome'. It was designed to teach us tactics such as challenging patrols from sentry position, observations, concealment, moving and keeping direction at night. The 'gruesome' part was for the amount of beastings received by their respective training teams.

Everything was introduced fairly rapidly because this was very basic soldiering. The 'buddy buddy' system was also explained. This is based on the 'you scratch my back and I'll scratch yours' maxim. Whilst in the field we were expected to work in pairs. So, for instance, when we had time for a meal, one of us would cook while the other one stayed alert. The theory was that it gave the opportunity to react against a hostile threat and generated good teamwork.

During Twosome we began to learn about moving at night. Most people can walk at night but to navigate and hide your whereabouts is very mind-testing and requires concentration and good map-reading skills.

One particular task our section was given was to move from various points around Woodbury Common and arrive back at our FRV (final rendezvous point). Physically this wasn't very testing but the pressure was tough, especially when I had to take my particular legs of the route. I didn't want to let the section down by getting us lost. To my surprise, and with a little luck, we made it back to the FRV, but one particular section managed to lose a man and we spent many hours of what could have been sleep looking for him. Naturally, we all paid the price in physical beastings from our training team when he was found safe and well.

This small episode had a major effect on the rest of the exercise because during the beastings that followed, we were covered from head to toe in cold wet mud. I was unable to clean my kit properly owing to my own cleaning kit becoming dirty, and I was likely to be picked up during a subsequent inspection. This would again result in another beasting, thus continuing the vicious circle. This was in fact a good learning process, because when I was lying in six inches of cold muddy water, holding a log at arm's length, it made me realise where I was going wrong! I decided in future to prepare my kit better by placing certain items into plastic bags before going into the field.

By now my body had started to become accustomed to the lack of sleep but, as expected, when I did manage to get

27

into some kind of troop harbour position for the night, we would be suddenly 'crash moved'. This simulated being attacked and tested our motivation to get moving and identify what was going on and how to react against it. Most of the time this meant firing our weapons and withdrawing to a temporary location in order for the troop and sections to reorganise. Thus personal preparation of our kit was again always important because it could be costly later if items were lost or left behind.

During Twosome I also experienced having the 'shits'. To most people this is not a major event when dealing with it in a home environment. But when the temperature is getting close to freezing and it's pitch black in the early hours of the morning, the sudden urge to have a crap is overwhelming. It was impossible to remove all the layers of clothing when the fast call of nature approached. On one particular night of Twosome I was close to tears just because I was literally shitting myself and couldn't do anything to stop it.

Twosome also gave us an insight into 'cam' and 'concealment', which I began to enjoy because this was what I had joined for and not all the bullshit. We spent a few lessons learning the art of making use of our local surroundings. When we thought we had put enough foliage on our equipment, half of the section went out and took up firing positions whilst the remainder attempted to spot them. Movement was the main thing that gave everyone away, not poor positions or inadequate camouflage as people first thought.

Come the end of this exercise, I was shattered, soaking wet and mentally drained. Strangely enough, though, I had begun to enjoy it and the thought of quitting had slipped away for the time being. At end ex (the end of an exercise) we had a short speed march back to camp, but luckily I never had any problems with this.

Back at camp, I was now sharing a six-man room with a number of other lads, but it would only be John and Trevor who would stay in it with me as we progressed through training. The troop morale had also started to rise as we began to settle into our new environment.

The lectures continued at a rapid pace, as did the physical training. The gym work remained extremely hard but for some reason I seemed to enjoy it now. Being fairly small, I had less body weight to throw around.

This wasn't the case with the Royal Marines BST (battle swimming test). Prior to joining up I had done very little in the way of swimming and found this event very testing. I was told to wear some old denim trousers, webbing which contained solid weights, and sling an old 303 rifle over my shoulder. Not a major problem, I thought.

This view drastically changed when the PTI told me to climb onto the *high* diving board, jump off, swim two lengths of the pool, tread water for two minutes, then take off the webbing and rifle and pass it to the instructor, who would be waiting at the side of the pool.

The jump off the board was the easy bit, trying to get back to the surface took a huge amount of effort. The kit and clothing seemed to pull me to the bottom of the pool. When I attempted to swim I found this extremely hard and needed to practise before I successfully completed the test. One particular lad, having jumped off the board, was unable to get back to the surface and I watched in horror as he was dragged out, coughing up water. I wasn't the only one in the troop finding the swimming difficult.

* * *

By now all the extra physical exercise had begun to increase my appetite and I was eating three large meals a day. The food was reasonably good and varied as long as I didn't find myself at the back of the queue. I enhanced these meals by eating lots of chocolate during the course of the day.

Most evenings I paid a visit to the Dutchy Bar, which was a fast-food caravan run by a civilian. Healthy eating was far from my mind and I didn't care what it was as long as it cured my hunger. The only problem caused by this luxury was when some of the lads, myself included, ran the risk of taking hot food back to the 'grots' (accommodation). Nine times out of ten we went undetected but on occasions the duty corporal managed to catch a few lads. Then all hell would break loose. In the morning the troop, or sometimes the individuals responsible, would be punished by either physical exercise or an extra parade of some description.

By the end of the fourth week I found that I had got over my bout of homesickness and had started to enjoy the challenges I was now facing. From this moment onwards there would be no looking back as I began to throw myself at the task of earning my Green Beret.

During our normal training day at CTCRM, weapons training was held at some point in the day. The main weapon I started with was the SLR or self-loading rifle. At the start of every working day everyone in the troop would go to the armoury at approximately 06.00 hours. We each had our own personal weapon, with a unique number to identify it when drawing it from the armoury. After the basic introduction to the weapon, it was then down to us to keep it clean and in good working order. Weapon inspections became routine daily events but, come the end of training, I had my own way of cleaning the different parts. The lecture on the SLR varied from marksmanship principles, to the theory of a group (group meaning a series of shots). On top of this, the loading, unloading and stoppage drills had to be perfected, whereupon our section corporals would then test them.

Once they were satisfied with our skills with the weapon, we took a trip down to the ranges near Exmouth. I really enjoyed this because it was my first real experience of firing live ammunition. Holding and firing a weapon like the SLR gave me a strange feeling of being very powerful. I cannot explain why I felt like this, but it was probably something to do with the knowledge of what this type of weapon could do!

The round fired through the SLR (7.62mm) is designed to stop a man in his tracks. The Falklands War, along with Northern Ireland, proved this time and again.

When a high-velocity round enters the human body it normally causes an entry and exit wound. The exit wound is not always directly behind where it entered the body. Bones have the tendency to deflect the round inside the body. So an entry wound in the arm could have an exit wound out of the shoulder. The round also travels at such a high speed that when it does enter and exit it creates a vacuum, causing dirt and clothing to be sucked with it, and thus more problems for the surgeon.

On the range we were tested on how well we performed. A lot of the tests incorporated various scenarios, which could vary from basic standing and kneeling position to a lying position, having run and fired from 200 yards away. The pressure to pass the final APWT (Annual Platoon

Weapons Test) was high. This affected me because near the end of a shoot I would be aware that I had dropped a couple of shots. The tendency to rush and snatch at the trigger was considerable, thus affecting my aim.

As the weeks sped I found that the troop was now gelling, even though our troop photograph showed a few more crossed-out faces. I began to feel a confidence growing, which prepared me mentally as well as physically for whatever they threw at me next. Our section had begun to work hard for each other, as had the troop. There was the odd occasion when there was a bit of friction between some of the lads but it never really lasted more than a day or two. That normally took the form of harsh words between individuals with the odd punch being thrown to resolve matters.

Come the end of the seventh week, our section had a change of instructor. Corporal Locke was a very quiet professional Marine and his presence seemed to give members of the troop vital confidence, me included. He rarely raised his voice but if he did give anybody a bollocking it would always be justified. It was his very presence that kept me from rapping on a hard load carry.

Exercise 'Hunter's Moon' began during the eighth week of the course and was designed to teach us new skills and enhance the ones we had already been shown. This included material I had been shown during my spells in the classrooms.

Hunter's Moon tested aspects of selecting routes by day or night, section firefight drills, target identification and judging distance.

The latter two seem rather minor but play a large part in section firefight drills. If a contact is made and the rest of the section cannot see the enemy, they will be unable to return proper direct fire, thus being no use whatsoever. It is a skilled task, demanding the ability to judge distances on bare features, which can only develop with experience. Factors like 'dead ground' make what you are looking at appear closer than at first thought. If sights on weapons are not set correctly then proper effective fire cannot be returned.

The days were long and hard and sleep was minimal, owing to the various night 'navixes' (yomps) and crash moves. The theory behind most of the exercises was that they were geared to test new tasks, like marching on a compass bearing, and monitor the skills we were now expected to know. The night navixes became harder in that the distances we were expected to cover increased, as did the difficulties in objectives set by the training team. These could be getting to RV points like pylons, stiles, or the edge of a wood. This wasn't a noticeable change because I was in fact learning to cope better with basic field craft; after a while it became second nature to me.

It was now well into week eight. The weather had began to deteriorate, with November bringing plenty of wet and frosty conditions. This makes life very uncomfortable for a soldier in the field and, because of this, many outward-bound type companies have designed equipment to improve living conditions. Unfortunately, we were not allowed to use items such as Gore-Tex or wear our own civilian walking boots. A lot of people disagreed with this method of thinking. If Marine recruits were prepared to buy equipment, then they should be allowed to use it. The main reason I believe we were not allowed to use our own kit in training was in a time of conflict we wouldn't know how to fight and survive with military-issued kit. What use would we be in a long conflict, when the loss of kit and daily wear and tear would mean that we could not get proper re-supplies of the lavish comfortable types?

The only protection I had from the elements during training was a pathetically worn-out green poncho, a standard-issue sleeping bag from the training store, which contained very little in the way of feathers, and the clothing I wore.

Nobody dared to complain about being cold as they would only be classed as wimps, and I certainly didn't want to give my instructors any reason to lash out another beasting.

By the end of the exercise I was again exhausted and completely soaked. One aspect which was stressed to me from the outset of training was that whilst operating in the field I had to look after my feet. If they started to give me problems then I would become a liability to the rest of the section. 'Trenchfoot' in the Falklands Campaign highlighted this problem when serving in the field for long periods.

At the conclusion of Hunter's Moon I had managed to maintain my feet rather well, especially as they had been very cold and wet for most of the exercise. This had been done by placing wet socks around my waist whilst yomping, thus drying them out. Then, when I had the opportunity to get my head down for an hour or so, I would put the dry socks back on after putting large amounts of talc over my feet. This important daily routine increased my morale; there is nothing worse than having sore feet to worry about when there are far more important things to be getting on with.

At end ex I quickly assisted in returning all the relevant

troop stores to the waiting four-ton truck. I was then informed that we were going on a load carry (yomp). The distance was never mentioned, so again it was all in the mind as to how far we had to go. After forming up in our sections with a full kit weighing about 60–80 pounds per man, we set off across Woodbury Common. The pace was quite fast and we were the leading section with the remainder of the troop following. The ground across the common was mainly tracks; these were rocky and covered with numerous deep pools varying in depth from about two inches to two feet. The most obvious thing to do when the section approached one of the deep-looking pools was to go around it; we soon learnt otherwise when the instructors screamed at us to go through them.

This was not a problem during the first couple of miles, but with a combination of rocky tracks, the extra weight and continuous pounding, my feet began to get very sore. The pain in my feet seemed to increase with every step, but at first I attempted to push it to the back of my mind. Mentally this appeared to work quite well, but changed dramatically when we left the common and went out onto tarmac lanes. What felt like an extremely hard road aggravated the problems with my feet and I began to feel blisters forming and skin coming away from my heels. The pain was horrendous and no matter how hard I tried to put it to the back of my mind, I couldn't. As well as having trouble with my feet I was endeavouring to stay with the pace, like everyone else in the troop.

After a considerable amount of time I began to have difficulties. My body started to tell me to stop. To my relief, I began to receive a bit of encouragement from a couple of the lads in the section as they seemed to sense I was beginning to struggle. Corporal Locke was also well aware of my condition and started shouting at me to keep on pushing. All I focused on was placing one foot in front of the other completely oblivious of my surroundings. The effort was numbing; all I could feel was my knees jarring, shins hurting, feet burning and my back and shoulders straining under the weight of the equipment. I don't know how long this state lasted or the distance I covered. Everyone in the troop had been suffering to a certain extent but I found it extremely tough going.

Fortunately, I managed to pull myself through the pain barrier and got back into the load carry successfully, completing it with the section and troop. To this day, I will never know how far we travelled or how I achieved it. The distance was irrelevant: the main hurdle that I had overcome on this particular yomp was going through the pain barrier, and knowing that if I tried hard enough I could push my body further than I thought.

Back in my room after returning all the exercise equipment, I took the opportunity to remove my high-leg combat boots and discover what state my feet were in. Shocked to say the least, I saw the skin around both heels had been completely rubbed away, exposing red tissue which continuously wept. The balls of my feet and the tops of my big toes contained the largest blisters I had ever seen. The treatment for this was extreme to say the least, and for three or four days I hobbled around the camp like an arthritic 90-year-old.

Of course it wasn't always work, and at weekends we were allowed to go on 'a run ashore' – a trip out normally associated with getting a few drinks down your throat. Nobody was allowed to leave camp unless they were wearing trousers, and everyone had to book out through the duty corporal guard commander. The leave period depended on how far through the training you were, so for us it began at about Saturday lunch time and ended at 23.00 hours, this being extended to about 03.00 hours towards the end of training. The rigmarole for booking out depended on the guard commander. If he wasn't too strict, then it was fairly straightforward getting the train, but if he was 'pussers' (by the book) then you could guarantee one of us would be sent back to change for not being smart enough to go on 'shore' leave.

When I did finally break free, I would normally go to either Exeter or Exmouth. I would spend the day buying various items and enjoying the freedom of being able walk around town. Then in the evening I would go for a drink or two. Although this was very relaxing, I couldn't really let my hair down because the thought of not getting back to camp on time was a worry and not worth the hassle that it would cause. Of course, not having a great deal of money was also a deciding factor. I only received approximately £45 a fortnight, and most of that was spent on chocolate and everyday items.

One particular Saturday I went into Exmouth with Mike and Phil and, after a few pints for encouragement, we stumbled into the local tattoo shop. We had been warned by our drill instructor not to get any tattoos whilst still in training, because of the risk of infection. With this warning at the back of our minds, we set about selecting our permanent reminders of our time in training. I didn't have any great yearning to have one, but it seemed like a good idea at the time, so, being a glutton for punishment, I received one to my upper right arm, which could be hidden by a T-shirt if required. Lots of the lads had 'Commando' or 'Blood

Groups' written on various parts of their anatomy, but I felt this wasn't right as I hadn't yet completed training. The pain didn't really bother me but it was rather tender for a few days after it was done.

Like everything else in the Marines, the drill instructor soon found out about a lot of lads having these tattoos and he was not too impressed about us ignoring his advice. I, too, should have listened because after a week or so I got a boil right under my tattoo, which was extremely painful and took a few weeks to heal.

I don't really think the tattoo was directly to blame for the boil, as I started to get them on my back and shoulders, some of which needed to be lanced by the sickbay medics. Quite a few lads got them whilst training and I personally believe this was because our bodies were run down and lacking in the vital vitamins required to keep us healthy.

Training continued, with new weapons being introduced. These were the 9mm sub machine gun (SMG) and the 7.62mm general purpose machine gun (GPMG). The SMG was a very basic weapon which had been in service for a long period of time, and the GPMG was a very powerful and rapid-firing section support weapon. The drills were to be learnt in depth as one GPMG would be taken per section on every subsequent exercise, yomp and speed march.

The weapon-training lessons were normally held daily, continually interspersed with lectures. Everything seemed to be happening very fast as we had also started to receive lectures on nuclear, biological and chemical warfare (NBC). The classroom became a very hard learning environment because tiredness often crept in when I sat in the lovely warm atmosphere. It was far easier to stay awake when running around the gym or doing practical weapons training.

Drill tests were carried out on all new weapons in the safe confines of the camp. Once these were completed, the troop spent a few days camped in wooden huts on Willsworthy Ranges in Dartmoor. The weather was extremely cold and wet for the time of year. Being exposed to these elements all day long made it very miserable when standing about waiting to get onto the firing point. The shooting itself was very good, and I especially enjoyed the night firing exercises assisted by the use of flares and other battle paraphernalia. The range we were using was an electric one where the targets came up at various distances between 100 and 300 metres. I soon found that in the dark of night, even with flares lighting up the sky, it was still very hard to spot and identify the targets.

I also carried out advance to contact drills, where we would patrol until we came under enemy fire. This was done alone, with an instructor setting me off along a gully and, as I progressed along the changing terrain, I had to identify and engage the targets as I went. This was a good scenario because not only did it test my observation skills but also my weapon handling. Other firing practicals that I carried out were firing the GPMG from the waist and live firing drills in full NBC kit. Other than being cold, wet and covered in boils, I thoroughly enjoyed my time at Willsworthy Ranges.

Once we were again back in the confines of camp, the lectures continued. We even started to receive lectures on Corps history. It became a regular thing to be tested on various aspects of the training as we progressed. One such test was on maths and English, commonly referred to as the NAMET test. This gave the Corps an idea of how suitable we were for potential promotion in the years to come. I didn't do particularly well in the test for one reason or another and I found that if I ever wanted to get past the rank of colour sergeant I would have to improve my education, especially in maths and English.

In the run-up to week 11 we were given lectures on survival skills. This entailed topics such as setting snares, water management and how to find and identify possible sources of food. At the conclusion of one of these lectures the section was presented with an extremely large white albino rabbit. Corporal Locke informed us that it was now the section responsibility to look after and feed the rabbit until further notice. It wasn't a real problem keeping and feeding the animal, but you could guarantee that when it came to rounds of the 'grot' the damn rabbit would either shit or piss somewhere. Sorry to say, we began to detest this rabbit. On one occasion, after we had returned from a signals exercise, John found that it had crapped on his bed and chewed one of his blankets. The rest of the section found this extremely amusing but John just couldn't see the funny side of it.

John soon had the last laugh because in week 11 we began exercise 'Dart Venture'. This was basically a survival exercise and started in camp, loading tents, cookers, food and camp beds onto the back of a four-ton truck. These stores unfortunately were for the training team and nothing to do with us. We had all been instructed prior to the exercise to make up a survival kit which was no larger than a tobacco tin. The training team then stripped us of our clothing, other than a pair of boots, underpants, shirt and survival tin. They then issued us with a set of overalls and instructed us to get onto the back of another empty four-ton truck.

After an hour or so of travelling we found ourselves being off-loaded in an isolated moorland spot. The time was somewhere near to midday and the weather was overcast, cold and very wet.

Standing in the rain and soaked to the skin in minutes, we shivered as the troop sergeant lectured us on the forth-coming exercise, setting the scenario that we were now on an escape and evasion type test. It was now down to our-selves to keep pushing through this week. I expected a hard time ahead.

I didn't realise at that time how right he was, it proved to be extremely tough. We were led along a riverbank and I couldn't help noticing how sodden everywhere was. Fountains of water were gushing from outlets in the grass banks.

The instructors informed us that we now had to look after ourselves until further notice, remaining tactical the whole time. We quickly teamed up. I was with John and a couple of other lads. Our first priority was to build a shelter of some description, because it was now getting dark and the tem-perature was falling quickly.

Searching the local surroundings, we managed to find a few fertiliser bags, which we attached to the roof of our wooden shelter. We also tried to gather wood, but every piece was soaked and absolutely useless for starting a fire.

Come nightfall, we had completed our shelter with the resources available and begun to settle down for what was going to be a long and cold night. Finding a comfortable position on the floor of our shelter, I huddled up with the

41

lads in an attempt to preserve precious body heat. Fatigue took over and I quickly dozed off.

I wasn't asleep long before I suddenly awoke shivering and shaking violently in my cold clothes. I was trembling uncontrollably and found myself gripping the lad next to me for warmth, knowing I had at least another 12 hours to go before daylight. Within minutes everyone was awake, moaning how cold they were. We whispered but the conversation was limited due to the inhospitable conditions. The rain still hadn't eased and I began to feel drips coming through the roof. The water had slowly built up on the plastic bags and seeped through any available hole.

Lying there dwelling on what I was doing to myself, I began to think of home. It was strange because my mind drifted onto everyday items like a kettle. I imagined what it would be like to pour myself a nice hot cup of sugary tea, or being able to walk into a warm, centrally-heated house and get into a red-hot bath. Moments like this made me realise how much I took for granted at home and the luxuries associated with it.

The minutes ticked by slowly and I was now very cold and close to the edge of my will to carry on. I realised that we were all suffering and it would take a team effort to get us through the night.

I began vigorously moving my toes in my boots in order to take my mind off how cold I was. This seemed to help for a bit but after a while I found I kept getting cramp in my feet and calf muscles. It became very easy just to lie there and try not to move. Every time someone moved in the shelter it seemed to aggravate the feeling of being cold. This night was probably the longest of my life; every second felt like an hour.

Dawn slowly arrived, but there was no let-up in the

drizzle. At last, to our great joy, the training team arrived. They came round and checked on us to establish what kind of night we had had. They seemed to find it very amusing when we gave them our response that we were 'fucking freezing'!

All I wanted to do now was get moving and generate some body heat. To my delight, we were instructed to get on and improve our living conditions.

The first objective was to get a fire going, but we only had one match each. Thus between us we had four matches and had to be extremely careful how we used them. We ensured we had the best possible kindling in order to get the fire started with the first match, but this was easier said than done as all the wood was soaking wet. Finally, with all our matches used, we managed to get a fire started, whereupon I set about making a brew of nettle tea. This small event of lighting a fire and attempting to make a consumable brew seemed to increase my morale.

One lingering problem I did think of, though: if the training team decided to move us, we had no means of lighting another fire.

During the remainder of the day we set snares and made ourselves as comfortable as possible. Come the dreaded nightfall and the first signs of being hungry, we were instructed to go back to the place where we had initially been dropped off. Once there, we were given maps, compasses and a route card marked with various checkpoints, and told that the training team would man some of the checkpoints. We were also given a safety 'Bergen' [rucksack], which contained the necessary stores and food to help us if we had a problem with an injury. The food in the Bergen was sealed and thus tamper-proof.

We set off against all the elements because it was now

very misty and wet. The yomp took us well into the early hours of the morning. I preferred doing this to shivering in our primitive shelters. Once at the FRV, we returned the stores and attempted to get some sleep. Unfortunately, though, after about 20 to 30 minutes my body had cooled off and thus I became extremely cold and unable to sleep again.

The exercise routine continued in this fashion for a few days. We would spend the day at our shelters and in the evening we would be sent off on a yomp. Due to the lack of food, each yomp became harder and my patience to catch food was running out. The river was in flood and therefore devoid of any fish, while the local rabbits were probably laughing, saying, 'Here's another bunch of those amateur recruits!'

On the morning of the fourth day I had become extremely hungry and felt I could eat almost anything! I sensed the majority of the troop were also beginning to feel the effects of starvation. Some individuals were moping around, losing any kind of motivation. Unfortunately, I wasn't the only one to notice this and the troop sergeant decided to get everyone together for a spot of morning PT. This started with a very mild circuit, which culminated next to the river. We were then instructed to strip to our underpants and get into the water and completely submerge. Bearing in mind we were now well into November, the shock of getting into and under the flowing water was distressing and my chest and lungs seemed to collapse like a rapidly deflating balloon. I began to hyperventilate, attempting to suck in any air that I could. My heart was pounding as if it was going to burst at any moment. Dragging myself from the river, I was left to gather my thoughts with the rest of the troop. I stared into the flames of the fire, searching for motivation and answers as to why I was doing this to myself. I decided I had to carry on and make the best use of my time. Somebody must have been listening to me, because the persistent rain had thankfully ceased for a while, giving me the opportunity to dry out a little.

That afternoon the training team returned with a large quantity of white rabbits. Amongst them was our section rabbit, which we had brought along at the beginning of the exercise. Corporal Locke gave us a few rabbits, whereupon he instructed us to 'have a feast'! We all lined up holding our rabbits by the back legs. I hit mine over the back of the head with the blunt side of my 'gollock' (knife). John seemed to take revenge on the section rabbit for the times he had had to change his bedding and replace the half-eaten blankets.

We had been instructed that punishment would be inflicted on any recruit causing unnecessary suffering to the animals. One of the lads broke into song: 'Run rabbit, run rabbit, run, run, run.' I found this thoroughly amusing, as did the rest of the troop, and I chuckled uncontrollably whilst preparing it for the pot. I didn't have any qualms about killing, skinning and eating the rabbit because of the experience of working on a turkey farm during my school days. I was also starving.

The stew itself was very bland and contained little in the way of ingredients other than the extra pieces of bone and gristle. It wasn't particularly appetising; however, it was hot food and assuaged my hunger pains. The stew kept me going for the remainder of the exercise, and after another yomp we were transported back to camp. I had lost a bit of weight but other than that I was fine.

Dark Venture had taught me a lot of good military skills, but more importantly it had taught me a great deal about myself. It made me appreciate small things in life, which I would have normally taken for granted. I also experienced real hunger and what it felt like to be self-sufficient whilst attempting to live off the land. It was far from easy.

We now started to use the assault course or 'bottom field' as it was known.

Battle fitness training (BFT) had begun.

The PTI introduced us to the assault course. It was done initially in loose order without any kit strapped to our bodies. He showed us each obstacle and demonstrated how we were expected to deal with it. We were then given the opportunity to master each one before we were put through our paces. The trickiest obstacle was the regain rope, which was securely attached between two points. I had to crawl across on my chest, stop halfway, hang down, then kick myself back up onto my chest and continue to the end of the rope. This was easier said than done, especially when I was wet, weighed down with kit and completely exhausted, because, after a few days of practice running around the course, climbing the 30-foot ropes and doing various other physical exercise, we were given the opportunity to do it whilst carrying our kit and rifles.

BFT developed into a morning routine of going down to the bottom field in order to improve our battle fitness. I found that every time I started to get ready for this period I became very nervous. I would get the shits and butterflies in my stomach, probably because I was apprehensive about what kind of session I would be put through.

The early starts were also cold and this would be aggravated when somebody in the troop failed to fill their water bottles correctly. Every morning the PTI lined us all out and

46

inspected our webbing, checking that our water bottles were filled to the rim. If anyone had failed to do this it resulted in the remainder of the troop getting a soaking in the water tank. On many occasions the troop broke the ice on the water tank even before we had started any fitness training on the assault course. This tested my resolve to keep pushing even when I was soaked and freezing cold. The ice-cold water also made the webbing heavier. My hands were unprotected, which increased the problem of holding onto the bars and ropes as we went around and around the course.

Each man had difficulties with one or another particular obstacle on the assault course, whether this was the 6-foot wall at the very beginning, the 'regain' rope or the 30-foot climbing rope.

Mine proved to be the 200-yard fireman's lift, carrying my kit and rifle, along with a colleague and his kit and rifle. This was always conducted at the end of a BFT session. We would be instructed to pair off with somebody similar in weight and size, but, being on the small side, I always ended up with somebody bigger than myself. Technique was important but the last 50 yards proved that brute force and determination were essential to complete it. I never failed this task but came very close on days when I wasn't feeling at my best.

Everybody in training had the odd day when for some reason or another they didn't perform as well as expected, but after a while I began to recognise the lads who struggled on a daily basis and were punished by the relevant PTI.

At the end of these sessions I found I would be shaking all over, owing to all the effort I had put in. This would be aggravated when we were given another 'tanking' (swimming in the large outside concrete water tanks) for not putting enough effort in as a troop. This angered me because the sudden shock of jumping back into the freezing water when very hot gave me headaches and seriously affected my breathing for a few minutes. But once back in a hot shower I soon forgot about the misery and pain that I had recently been through and carried on from where I had left off.

By now the training syllabus was rapidly coming to the halfway point – week 15. I had successfully completed the gym work along with the BST and now felt very settled in this training environment. As a result of this success I was rewarded when the training team elected me to be a section commander for the remainder of the training. This gave me extra responsibilities, though I really didn't need to have these. I was beginning to enjoy myself and was quietly confident, so I jumped at the chance. I was now expected to make decisions when required, especially when in the field and away from the training team. Certain individuals in the section were always quick to challenge my decision, especially when map-reading on yomps. When Marines are 'chin strapped' (tired) they always hate going any further than is absolutely necessary.

It took me a while to get used to this leadership role that I had been given. Anyone can tell someone what to do, but you have to earn people's respect. It is not until you have achieved this that it becomes easier to get them to work for you.

During week 14 we embarked on a test exercise called 'Baptist Run'. It was designed to test all our field-craft skills, from map-reading, to camouflage and concealment.

Before the start of this exercise, the troop officer lined the whole troop out on the football field opposite the training centre, where he inspected every recruit. This in itself caused problems, because it was absolutely blowing a 'wholly' (gale) and throwing it down. We had to empty everything out of their waterproof containers and place it onto our ponchos so he could see we had all the relevant kit. By the time the inspection was complete, everything from my spare socks to my powdered toothpaste was saturated.

This exercise began with yet another load carry up to Woodbury Common, where we began practising our field-craft skills. Throughout the whole of this exercise the weather was appalling, and on one night when we had a brief opportunity to have a brew and a chat, it seemed from the conversation that morale was extremely low. Some of the lads were talking about quitting. One lad called Stone from Southend was in serious pain. He was very determined and had the character to keep going when times got really rough. Throughout the exercise he was complaining about how sore his feet were after all the yomping, but still he pushed himself to his limit. During this exercise he did better than some of the others from the troop.

At end ex and on our return to camp, Stone went straight to the sickbay to get his feet checked. Baptist Run turned out to be his last ever exercise because he was found to be suffering from severe frostbite in his toes. His subsequent attempts at rehabilitation in Hunter Troop failed, which resulted in him being medically discharged from the Marines. Stone was not alone as a lot of good men fell by the wayside due to injury whilst in training. The mental and physical pressures to keep going in training after an injury required a considerable amount of extra effort.

*   *   *

With Baptist Run successfully completed, the troop now had the fifteenth week passout parade and Christmas leave to look forward to. This passout parade was to give the lads the opportunity to show their parents around the place. It also signified the beginning of Commando training on our return from leave.

A few members of my family came down to see me participate in a demonstration of unarmed combat, gym work, BFT and a parade. We were then sent on leave, being warned not to forget our fitness training whilst celebrating the festival fun!

Once home, it felt very strange, as if nothing at all had changed other than myself. A lot of the lads I had been at school with suddenly appeared immature, and I found their lifestyle mundane compared with the pressures at CTCRM. At the end of Christmas leave I was, strangely enough, looking forward to returning and getting on with the remainder of my training.

The journey back by train was now becoming second nature and before long I was unpacking in my grot with the rest of the lads, who were returning in dribs and drabs during the course of the night. We exchanged stories of our exploits whilst on leave, and it soon felt as if we had never been away. Some lads, however, were completely different – going on leave had made them realise how much they had missed home, friends and the civilian lifestyle which had been abruptly taken away from them 15 weeks earlier. It was during this period after Christmas leave that we lost a high number of lads from the troop.

With the early morning call we were brought back to the CTC way of life, only to discover that we were now out of

50

the Plymouth Company and into our new company, Chatham. To us this signalled a change from the basic training phase to Commando training.

4

CHATHAM COMPANY

After the break, it didn't take long to get back into the motivated attitude of a Royal Marine recruit. The lectures became slightly more complex, introducing battle tactics and sops (standard operational procedures).

Unfortunately, like all classroom concepts, the theory needed to be put into practice.

Patrolling and signals work were normally carried out around the camp and on numerous trips to Woodbury Common. All kinds of hurdles were encountered, especially on the patrolling practices. Road junctions, stiles and isolated buildings were dealt with as a patrol to give cover as we passed. Hand signals caused many problems for the section, under the watchful eye of Corporal Locke.

The instructors expected us to learn quickly. It was down to us to rectify our own errors and shortcomings. If we didn't then the training team would inflict the appropriate punishment.

They also expected us to always remain tactical and alert. This added to the pressure of getting it right, especially when soaking wet after days of hard patrolling.

We learned the methods and procedures on observation points (OPs), which were mainly dependent on the type of intelligence required. This ranged from planning how to enter and exit a position when close to the enemy, to the problem of going for a crap, sealing it in a bag and taking it with you when vacating a position.

My own experience of OPs was that they were extremely testing. Not only did I have to cope with feeling cold, due to the lack of movement, I also found it psychologically hard to keep my concentration level at a maximum.

When it came to the signals or communication lectures, I soon realised that the theory was the easy part; once out on the ground it quickly became a different matter. Voices over the radio net seemed harder to understand, and when the pressure intensified it also became harder to decipher the coding system that we used.

The section and troop radios were also hard work, especially when combining patrol skills, map-reading skills and correct radio procedures.

Before long, 'Silent Night', had begun. This exercise took place on Woodbury Common, where we were shown military skills, which incorporated working professionally as a team. As with all the previous exercises, I had very little in the way of rest. The section and troop continued with the patrolling skills, moving tirelessly from one place to the next. I learnt how to give a full set of orders in relation to carrying out a patrol and how to use the best of the local surroundings. For instance, I used branches and twigs to illustrate what an area looked like from the information taken from a map.

We patrolled all day in the section without a let-up in the hostile wet and windy weather. Then in the evenings we carried out orders in relation to planning and executing an ambush or other type of patrol. The night-time tasks tested how I worked and planned the operation with the section.

These tasks varied considerably, from fighting patrols to CTRs (close target recces). They normally took up most of the night, so sleep deprivation made it extremely hard, especially as the week progressed.

Strangely enough, I had now started to get used to the feeling of being wet whilst working in the field. The extra pressure didn't really give me the time to stop and think about being cold and miserable. But I had many moments when I suddenly thought, What am I doing it for?

One thing I had started to notice now was that we were working well as a team. The troop was fairly settled and the camaraderie seemed to make it all come together. The section and troop also shared in everyone's own personal strengths; when I did reach a down point during the exercise, there was always someone in the team to get me motivated again.

Eventually I made it to the end of the exercise, where I had the unexpected pleasure of getting a lift back to CTCRM in a four-ton truck. One thing that I did not relish, though, was the jump off the back. After nearly a week in the field with wet and battered feet, the pain from the four-foot drop from the tailgate was fearful.

Back at CTCRM, another topic that I took time to think over was NBC (nuclear, biological and chemical warfare). Over the period of one week, the troop spent a considerable amount of time in the classroom learning about this type of warfare. I was taught how to identify the signs and symptoms of an NBC attack and the use of the large amount of extra equipment to deal with it.

The theory was then again put to the test in various places around the camp, including a trip to the CS gas chamber.

This was a small brick building, which had been designed to store ammunition and could hold about six to eight people in one go. During my time at CTC, when marching to the parade ground I had seen other recruits leaving the chamber in all kinds of distressed states. This fueled my speculation about what really happened inside.

The chamber was to be an introduction in how to use our equipment within a controlled environment. Using CS gas as the punishment, should anyone get the drills wrong? I wondered.

So, come the day of the chamber, I lined up outside with the remainder of the troop and waited patiently for what lay ahead. Unfortunately, I wasn't the first to enter. All I could do was watch and wait for the first few members of the troop to go in.

After a while and without warning a couple of the lads came bursting out, choking and vomiting. It was at this point that I noticed none of them had their masks on as they came out into the fresh air. Eventually, they were all out, and appeared to be suffering from the same symptoms: gasping for breath and in a semi-collapsed condition.

I now felt very anxious and wanted to ask them what had happened in the chamber. Unfortunately, before I could do this, my section was called forward.

The corporal in charge instructed us to put our respirators on. Once this was done we checked off in pairs to confirm we were correctly dressed and that the mask had a correct seal around our faces. When we were all satisfied with ourselves, we entered the chamber.

Inside it was dark and slightly claustrophobic. There was also a very eerie feeling in the air as the instructor lit another CS gas tablet, causing a large white cloud to engulf us all. My senses went into overdrive as I consciously breathed inside my respirator. The instructor then began to give us tasks to complete. The first one was the standard drinking drill.

Like all drills, it required precision rather than speed, which generally caused panic if a slight error was made. Removing the mask and shutting my eyes, I poured the water into my mouth from the black plastic water bottle I had been carrying on my webbing.

Fortunately, I got it right. After replacing my mask, I exhaled in order to clear any contaminated air which could have still been inside my respirator. One or two lads did get it wrong, as they began to cough and splutter once their masks were back on. We quickly continued with the various drills, which included eating dried biscuit and decontamination tests. Once I had successfully completed the tasks, I was told to remove my mask, take a breath in and shout out my name and number. Within an instant of removing it, I felt an immediate burning sensation in my throat and eyes. My lungs collapsed as if I was suffering from some kind of asthma attack.

It was very distressing. I couldn't breathe or speak due to the amount of vomiting I was doing. I didn't even manage to say my name before I was literally thrown out of the chamber by the scruff of my neck. The relief of the outside air slowly revived my ability to function properly.

This experience highlighted the importance of carrying out the drills correctly. However, I devoutly hoped I would never have to fight or survive in this kind of environment.

The pace of the training was now intense and all kinds of weapons were being introduced, such as the hand grenade.

The weapon itself was very basic in design, and it was just like throwing a stone.

After throwing the practice grenades, learning about detonators and killing areas of the weapon, the troop went off to the 'Meg range' on the common.

This was a system of trenches designed to protect the occupants from any fragmentation. At the starting point the troop sat in a bunker, waiting to be called forward to the throwing point. The instructors were at the various safety and ammunition points around the range. We were to be called one by one to the arming point, then proceed to the throwing point, throw two grenades and move to the finish bunker.

I waited patiently in the bunker for my turn to throw and listened to the muffled shouts of 'GRENADE!' This was followed by a few seconds of silence before the explosion. It wasn't particularly loud but it sent a shock wave through the bunker, hammering home the reality of what this weapon was capable of doing. After a while I received my call to go forward, so, leaving the safety of the bunker, I moved to the ammunition point. I was handed a grenade. Carefully I avoided touching the detonator. The heat from your hand can sometimes activate it so I placed it anxiously into the green egg-shaped housing. I proceeded along the trench, where I met the throwing instructor. He asked me if everything was OK, and I informed him that I was fine. Underneath, though, I felt a little apprehensive about throwing this potentially lethal weapon.

I got on with the drill and threw the two grenades one at a time, shouting and ducking for cover after each throw. Then I moved to the second bunker, where I waited for the remainder of the troop to complete their throwing.

Most of the day was spent hanging around and, by the

afternoon, the majority of the lads had thrown their grenades. Whilst waiting to be called forward from the safety of the bunker, I began to listen to the training team moving around outside the trench.

The sounds of people moving around all day had been quite distinctive because of the general restrictions of movement on the range. Then, suddenly, there seemed to be a panic. I heard the sound of someone falling over, quickly followed by a very close explosion. The blast shook straight through the bunker, raising a dust cloud and creating instant silence. Grit and dust were everywhere. It didn't take me long to surmise what had happened. Judging from the worried shouts that followed, somebody had dropped a live grenade within the confines of the range.

Staring around the bunker, I tried to establish if anyone from the troop could have been outside and involved in the commotion. No one seemed to be missing.

After a few moments there appeared to be calm. Several of the training team had been shouting, 'ARE YOU ALL RIGHT?' Somebody shouted back to say everyone was fine and that nobody was injured. The urgency in their voices clearly indicated that something had happened.

My mind continued to race. Who could have dropped the grenade?

Shortly after this chaos, we were called out from the bunker and awaited the instructions to move back to camp. At this point, the troop lieutenant appeared, and from his dress and the fact that he was covered in mud it didn't take long to deduce that he was the one who had dropped the grenade. He seemed to be a little shaken and quickly disappeared after a few words to us. I later found out that he had somehow dropped the grenade at the throwing point and the corporal there had pushed him out of the way into a blind spot in the trench, saving the life of the troop officer. Back at camp and on the verbal advice from the troop sergeant, no one in the troop ever mentioned this event again.

By now, the 'bottom field' experience had become a ritual. Every morning I would find myself plunging into freezing water.

At the conclusion of charging tirelessly around the assault course many times, I would always find myself being instructed to climb the 30-foot ropes for one last effort. The 30 pounds of wet kit and rifle seemed to drain every last drop of my strength.

We spent another week live firing, but this time it was at Okehampton camp on the edge of North Dartmoor. Live firing section attacks were totally different from the ones I had been used to using blank ammunition. The sound was greatly increased, and this added to the confusion as it was impossible to communicate. I also had the opportunity to fire the 'Carl Gustav', or 84mm anti-tank weapon. This was an experience in itself because the power generated in this hand-held weapon was immense.

Whilst live firing at Okehampton, the physical beastings from the training team continued without let-up, and after an exhausting day of section attacks, we would then speed march (run) back to the camp.

The speed marches were always carried out in full webbing, carrying self-loading rifles. The distances we covered were anything from four to ten miles. I personally found the speed marches easier than some of the harder yomps. I think this was probably because I enjoyed running. The stress created on my shins was always the same, *painful*! On an uphill gradient during the speed marches, we would always break into quick time (fast walk). I didn't really enjoy this method and would have preferred to have continued running up the gradients because of the extra stress created on my shins. I cannot really remember the exact reason why we did this but the ten-minute-mile pace was always expected.

The week live firing on Dartmoor turned out to be very wet, but I did manage to get a night out in Okehampton with a few of the lads. This was spent drinking as much beer as possible in the short time we had to discover the nightlife that didn't seem to exist in midweek.

The live firing section and troop attacks always raised the adrenaline levels but we eventually found ourselves back at CTCRM.

On our return, we began learning about defensive positions and tactics. I was shown how to dig and conceal a proper defensive trench position, learning how to make it strong, comfortable and capable of withstanding shelling.

The lectures were given prior to another exercise I was about to embark on.

Exercise 'Holdfast' was designed to test the troop's ability to move into a defensive position and dig in. The instructors would then test our NBC drills whilst we were in the field.

The exercise started with a load carry up to and around Woodbury Common. The troop also carried the support weapons that we had now learnt to use, the GPMGs and the 84mm anti-tank weapons. These extra weapons were passed amongst us as we yomped, in order to share the burden of the extra weight.

Eventually it came to my turn to carry either the GPMG or 84mm. I put the sling of the 84mm over the back of my neck so the weapon was in front of me as I marched. At first the extra weight on the front of my body seemed to counter-balance the Bergen (rucksack) and webbing that I was carrying on my back. This feeling quickly vanished after a few hundred yards and the comfortable sling over my neck rapidly turned into a hot piece of barbed wire cutting into the flesh of my neck. The pace of the yomp was rapid and the amount of physical pressure on my body was excruciating. The strength in my muscles evaporated rapidly and the pain from the extra weight caused spasms to race down my spine. Eventually, somewhat the worse for wear, as darkness fell the troop reached its destination on the common.

To my relief, I was then told to ditch my Bergen in order to make a recce for a good location for the troop to dig in. Five or six of us moved off and, after a short patrol, the troop sergeant told me where he wanted my section to go.

Identifying the ground, I returned to RV with the rest of the section and gave a short briefing on what was going to happen.

Once we were in the defensive location, I indicated to the remainder of the lads where we were required to dig in. After this I paired off with a guy called Kirk and began to dig our new home.

The going was very tough owing to the rocky ground on the common. My shattered muscles from the recent load carry didn't make it any easier and I quickly began to get blisters on my hands. The night progressed slowly but we made the extra effort to get finished because the training team expected us to be in by first light.

In the morning the troop officer and the remainder of the training team visited us. They began to give us advice on how to make our trenches as comfortable as possible. From then on, we were never left alone.

It began with mock attacks every other hour forcing us to remain alert. This continued throughout the night and the only sleep I did manage to get was a catnap here and there. A sentry routine was arranged, but when an attack came, the whole troop had to stand to.

During the second day we received our first simulated chemical attack, namely CS gas, which forced us into the NBC phase of the exercise. At first it seemed easy coping with the extra strain but as the hours wore on, the mental stress of wearing a respirator increased. The S8 respirator contained a breathing valve which made a slight popping sound every time you breathed in and out. This popping noise began to drive me insane and I was unable to concentrate on anything else. Sleeping with it on my face became impossible.

The NBC phase lasted about a day and a half and was extremely tiring, compounded by the fact that I was standing in 12 inches of muddy water. My feet were extremely cold and sore and the rest of my body was soaking wet. My morale was now at a very low point, but I didn't feel like quitting. I was getting conditioned to the harshness of soldiering and began to look at the funny side of things. This was somewhat out of character for me. I believe this may have been a major turning point in how I began to look at life and put certain things into perspective.

Mentally drained owing to lack of sleep, I found it very easy to daydream and switch off. Fortunately, we started to go out on patrols, which gave me an escape from our water-filled trench. The patrols were always carried out at night.

We were expected to perform them professionally, which included a debrief about the patrol on our return.

The very first patrol of this particular exercise ended up with us having a contact with our target. During this, a number of punches were actually thrown in the chaos that ensued. Kirk even managed to get his weapon snatched from him by one of the training team, which didn't go down too well in the morning. They told us, after a severe bollocking, that it was due to a lack of aggression and moral fibre.

Eventually, after about six days, we were ordered to withdraw from our trenches. Even this turned out to be an effort, in that we had to fill them in whilst remaining tactical. Once this was done, we carried out a proper tactical withdrawal to find it developing into yet another yomp.

Starting off, the first mile or so didn't seem to be a problem. However, a week in the trench and severe lack of sleep began to take its toll on me. Time ticked by as the section progressed though the lanes. I began to pick out points along the way to aim for, such as a distinctive tree or a gap in the hedge. I had no idea how far we were going so I just kept pushing myself, until I was nearly hallucinating.

The training team was always nearby but there was never a time when they would do a lot of shouting. It was down to me, so I had to keep working hard in order to make it back to CTC. Some of the troop were less fortunate and found themselves in the back of the 'rap wagon' (the safety vehicle that followed at the back of a yomp).

By the time I reached the gates of CTCRM I was in pieces. My feet had lumps of soft white skin tissue falling from them, and my shoulders and hips were covered in sore, pus-filled abrasions. The pain was horrendous when I tried to get in the shower and sleeping felt like something from the past.

63

*   *   *

It took me a number of days to recover fully from exercise 'Holdfast', but the pace of the training didn't let up.

We started helicopter drills and bayonet fighting on the rifle ranges just outside Exmouth. The bayonet training was taken extremely seriously because many of the instructors had seen at first hand how important this type of combat was in the Falklands campaign. Controlled aggression was the key, but physical stamina was also required as I underwent various obstacles involving dummy targets.

It was during this day that I had my first taste of a game called 'murder ball'. The game had no rules other than you had to score in the opposing team's goal. It was played with a full bottle of water and would always result in an injury of some kind. This kind of game may have been frowned upon but it created a tremendous spirit amongst the troop.

Unfortunately, our team lost the game, but I got off lightly compared with the others as I came away sporting only a black eye.

During a break in the programme, the training team sometimes enjoyed playing their own little games. This nearly always involved members of the troop carrying out various tasks. One such task was given to a lad called Nash who had had a bad day for one reason or another.

Every member of the troop was instructed to take off his woolly jumper and hand it to Nash. He was then told to put all the jumpers on! After something of a struggle, we managed to get about 15 or so jumpers over his own. It was all light-hearted and Nash had begun to sweat profusely.

Looking like the Michelin man, Nash was then told to run down to the butts at the target end of the range and back again. Bearing in mind it was a fairly warm and sunny day, he returned from the 600-metre jog looking as if he had just completed the London Marathon. I had a good laugh at Nash's expense along with the rest of the troop, but it was moments like this that raised morale and kept a good spirit going. Eventually Nash saw the funny side of it, once he had recovered and cooled down.

Most evenings were spent in the accommodation block cleaning and preparing kit. Throughout the night, various styles of music could be heard as you moved around. One of the most frequently heard records at the time was quite aptly named 'When the Going Gets Tough'! Needless to say, it became the troop theme tune, being slightly changed by the PTI to 'When the going gets tough, the wimps fuck off to sickbay!'

Certain individuals in the troop would always make excuses as to why they continually failed to keep up in speed marches or lagged behind on the bottom field. Sprained ankles, shin splints and Achilles tendons were the most common excuses. Fortunately, the Navy sickbay medics had heard them all before. Everybody was now carrying an injury, especially as we were heading towards the Commando tests.

The weeks were closing rapidly on the end of training and this was indicated when we were issued with the cap comforter, the traditional Commando woollen hat – the type worn by those who served under Sir Winston Churchill in the Second World War.

This headgear meant we were now in the Commando testing phase of training. It also meant, because it was the tradition of the Corps, we double marched (ran) everywhere around the camp.

I felt confident in my ability, and my physical fitness was

improving daily. The only thing I was concerned about was whether I picked up an injury of some kind.

The training team also identified my confident attitude towards the course and made me a section diamond (commander). This gave me extra responsibilities leading a section through the final weeks of training, which included the final exercise and Commando tests. The role really didn't have any specific benefits but it did give me the opportunity to lead and make decisions.

The training was still very intense and part of every day was spent on the assault and Tarzan courses.

The Tarzan course consisted of high wire obstacles designed to test individual nerves at height. It started with an 80-foot death slide, followed in succession by ten other obstacles ranging in height and technique. The distance over the 13-minute course wasn't particularly long but it required concentration and a huge amount of bottle. We were also expected to carry our standard webbing order – 22 pounds plus SLR.

Owing to my size, I didn't seem to have any major problems with the Tarzan course. It was different for others, though. Week in, week out, it always seemed to be the same lads struggling around it.

I had always suffered from slight bouts of vertigo when placed in high, vulnerable positions. Nevertheless, I quickly learned to overcome this problem, courtesy of the Mountain and Arctic Warfare Cadre.

The Cadre, as it is known in the Corps, is responsible for training MLs (mountain leaders). They are experts in mountain and arctic warfare, cliff assaults and survival techniques. The MLs have a peacetime role teaching the remainder of the Corps their skills.

One cold, wet and windy morning we arrived at an

isolated quarry in the middle of Dartmoor. The quarry had rock faces ranging from between 40 and 70 feet in height. At the top and bottom of these cliffs were flat areas ideal for training. There was also an icy-cold pool of water where frantic digging had once taken place when the quarry had been in full production.

The day was spent practising various climbing and abseiling techniques. I was also shown how to construct a roller pulley system designed to get men and equipment up cliff faces. It was a day of testing nerves and showing the rest of the troop you had a bit of bottle. The MLs were extremely professional and would expect us to do only what they themselves would do. Listening to the instructions was also an essential feature when preparing our kit.

It eventually came to the test I had been waiting for, 'the run downs'. This was a faster way to abseil but defied the normal human concept of how to go down the rock face. Most climbers tend to abseil by walking backwards over the lip of a cliff and then sit back into the rope, controlling the descent with either left or right hand. The run down, however, was completely different. It entailed walking straight over the lip of the cliff so that you were facing the ground. It took great courage to do this and stay on your feet.

My time had come. Connecting myself to the rope with my carabina, I went forward with my heart in my mouth.

'Away you go' were the last words I heard as my mind focused on what I was supposed to be doing. The first shock I had was when I realised how hard it was to feed the rope into the carabina around my waist. Coming to terms with this, I approached the edge of the cliff. My fear vanished and the adrenaline raced around my body as I tried to lock my knees and keep my body straight. It was the most unnatural experience as I shakily stepped over the lip of the cliff.

Immediately, I came face to face with the brakeman who was controlling my descent 50 feet below. My life was in his hands!

I then attempted to run down the rock face. Just as I was getting into my stride, the brakeman pulled on the rope, stopping me halfway down. I halted instantly. At least the brake system worked properly.

I was now suspended on the rope.

The ML below shouted, 'Let go of the rope!'

Facing the choice of either letting go or swimming the icy pool when I got to the bottom, I let go of the rope.

'Right. Now touch your head!'

Grabbing the back of my helmet, I soon realised that I had lost my fear of heights.

Nash was not so fortunate. On his descent the rope suddenly became caught in his combat jacket and the carabina. He was stuck by his waist 30 feet in the air!

He spent 15 minutes dangling like a puppet from his waist and turning blue, all because he had not carried out the instructions. He was eventually cut from the rope after being secured to another safety rope.

Just as I was getting into the swing of being back at CTC, the troop was whisked off to Poole in Dorset. The atmosphere at Royal Marines Poole was really laid back compared with life at CTC.

RM Poole was where we would learn and develop skills to be used on amphibious operations. We had various lectures on the types of boat we were going to encounter. This included LCUs and LCVPs (landing craft).

Landing craft are designed to get men ashore in relatively large numbers, and are slow and extremely uncomfortable when travelling long distances. The LCVP can carry 30 fully laden Marines or a Land Rover and trailer. The LCU can transport up to a company of Marines with kit or a Bedford four-ton truck.

As we practised different types of landings with the LCVPs, I soon found it wasn't very amusing being dumped short of the beach whilst carrying all my kit. I got quite a shock when stepping from the ramp to suddenly find myself in six feet of ice-cold water. The training team and coxswains found the sights rather amusing at times, but our professionalism was always required.

From the LCUs we moved to the rigid raiders and inflatable Geminis (ribs). These small boats were used for different types of operations.

The raiders were robust and made of fibreglass. They were used for transporting and deploying a section of men quickly. The ribs were inflatable wooden-bottomed boats that could also carry a section of men. These were perfect for covert infiltrations or extractions on isolated waters.

The drills were far more exciting but the feeling of being cold and wet remained. We practised silent approaches to fast run-ups where the coxswain would charge at full speed towards the beach (in a raider) and at the last moment pull the outboard engine from the water. The raider would race up the beach, carrying us some 20 to 30 yards from the water's edge.

The drills were not only about insertion; we also practised extraction drills from the beach.

When the surf was big, the section waded out towards the incoming raider and stood in pairs about one boat's width apart; the coxswain manoeuvred the boat into the gap until we managed to grasp the side. It then became a physical struggle to keep the raider still and facing the incoming surf.

At this point, it was potentially very dangerous because of the outboard engine on the raider. A knock on the head could also have proved fatal in the water. Once the boat was reasonably steady we would climb into it two at a time, leaving the pair holding the front of the boat until last.

Cross decking drills (transferring from the LCVPs to raiders) also contained an element of danger, especially when the sea had a bit of a swell. On one occasion after loading ourselves onto one of the LCVPs with all our equipment, we set off for a designated rendezvous with the raiders. The sea was rough, which became even more apparent when the raider drew up next to our craft. Once the boats were together and running parallel, we began to cross deck into the raider. This was easier said than done as the two craft were moving up and down in the water. The wake from the LCVP aggravated this movement, especially when we were standing up and attempting to pass our bergens over, and spray from both boats made the surfaces treacherous underfoot.

We repeated the drill time and again, making sure we actually got into the raider, in the right positions, with the GPMG gunner at the front so he would be able to put down covering fire if required on landing. And every time I practised the drills I made a conscious effort not to place my fingers between the two boats to prevent them from being crushed.

The week at Poole was the build-up to the final exercise, 'Sea Sting', which was designed to test and put into practice all the skills we had been taught throughout recruit training.

This was now the beginning of the test phase and I

70

received a briefing on the first operation of Sea Sting. The troop officer giving it split the details of the raid into separate phases. As the briefing lasted a considerable time, I made many notes in my waterproof pad while attempting to commit all the extra details of the operation to memory.

Once the boss had finished, he asked me to explain and go over the deployment part of the operation. This covered who was going in what boat and where and when everyone deployed on the ground. I had to know what my section was going to do and be aware of what the other sections were doing, and where. If there were going to be any questions from any of the lads before setting off, I needed to know the answers.

The planned operation was a dawn assault using the ribs to take us to a location near to Portland breakwater. From here, in our sections, we were to move across to a disused fort, where a dawn attack would be mounted.

Timings, as in any kind of military operation, were critical. Failure to keep to these timings could result in an array of problems, from missing a high tide to not being able to give proper covering fire to another section.

Although this was a training exercise it was treated extremely professionally.

I was now under pressure to make sure that everything went to plan because if I fucked up the whole troop raid could turn to rat shit.

After the troop briefing I went over our mission with the rest of the section in order to clarify what was required should anything happen to me. We took time to rehearse the phases of the operation, walking it through in slow time so that everyone knew what was going to happen during the operation.

I then had a few hours to kill, which were spent preparing my kit. I double-checked it in anticipation for the week that lay ahead. I knew exactly what I needed, through trial and error on the previous exercises during training.

Sea Sting was a pass or fail test where the training team would be watching and monitoring our every move. Naturally, I was very determined to pass, and only an injury of some kind would prevent me from doing so. I wasn't going to be back-trooped at this stage of training.

Before starting the exercise Corporal Locke took the section to one side and explained that the training team was not looking for supermen; all they wanted to see was plenty of enthusiasm and motivation, especially when it got tough. We were all expected to keep going and not switch off because, in reality, it could cost lives.

At about 02.30 hours on a cold spring morning we set off in the ribs. The section was split between two boats. The whole troop was moving off at intervals and we were the second section to go. I was now completely focused on what I was doing.

The weather was dry and overcast as we left, which made for a calm sea. This began to change slightly as we got further out and my dry combats soon became sodden from the spray over the front of the rib.

After an hour of being tossed around in the vulnerable rib, we slowly approached Portland breakwater. The cold sea wind and icy water made me feel yet more uncomfortable. I tried to ignore this and concentrated on my map-reading skills in order to identify landmarks close to the drop-off point (DOP). I got my bearings and orientated myself to the shoreline.

When I had satisfied myself that we were in the right location, the coxswain turned the engines off. Silently, we began to paddle towards the shore. I quickly discovered how time-consuming this was as we battled against the invisible current. I continually scanned the shore as we slowly approached the rocky outcrop where we intended to disembark. I couldn't see anything. All I could hear was the crashing noise of the waves as they broke against the rocks. My mouth had gone slightly dry and I could feel my breathing intensify as the adrenaline around my body began to increase.

The last few metres between the rib and the rocks closed rapidly with the assistance of the waves. The inflatable side of the rib bounced against the rocks but, before I had time to think, the section was dashing from the boat. The first man out attempted to hold the boat steady. The remainder of the section took up fire positions, covering around the front of the boat. We quickly removed our life jackets, passing them back to the last man, who then threw them back into the rib and signalled for the coxswain to withdraw to the relative safety of the open sea.

Checking my watch, I gave the order to move and we set off for the next objective.

I was towards the front of the patrol, which gave me the opportunity to check where I was taking the section. This also enabled me to keep control if the situation or the ground changed. I felt reasonably satisfied that the section was now prepared for any eventuality. We had been told during the briefing to expect enemy patrols to be moving close to the fort. Eventually, after a few scares but no contacts, we reached the final RV and moved into all-round defence.

Our mission in the assault was to press through a disused fort, clearing the various buildings on the ground floor as we went. Another section would then clear the upper floor simultaneously whilst the third section gave covering fire.

Once the objectives had been taken, the third section would move down to the jetty and secure it for a fast pick-up by raiders.

It was now a case of waiting for the signal to start moving forward. Our communications were established by clicking on the radio net to signify that we were all in position for the assault.

I would have much preferred to start the attack straight away because, with my wet clothing, I began to get cold as my body started to cool. However, everything was going to plan because no contacts had been made with the enemy by any of the troop.

At about 05.30 hours we moved off in accordance with our briefing. This was confirmed by yet another rapid succession of clicks on the radio net.

No sooner had we got to our feet than right on cue a flare shot straight into the air, lighting up the night sky. The covering section started to put down simulated fire and we then began to fire and manoeuvre into the buildings. The noise was deafening and we quickly began to fight our way through the fort.

Speed, aggression and control were the ingredients of proper house-clearing drills. To assist in making it more realistic lots of thunder flashes (simulated grenades) were thrown.

I began systematically to clear the building by bursting through doors firing my weapon from the waist.

A thunder flash suddenly exploded.

In the confines of the room the sound echoed in my ears and momentarily stunned me. Spellbound by deafness, I felt as if I was in my own little world and my perception of what was happening changed for a brief second. I couldn't hear a thing, other than muffled screams. Unable to establish why, I began to study detail around me from the large, thick walls of the old decrepit fort to the puddles of murky stagnant water covering the floor within the room.

Suddenly, after a number of long seconds, the spell I was under vanished and the ringing in my ears faded. Pulling myself together, I saw that the room was empty so automatically I shouted, 'Room clear!'

We progressed rapidly through the fort and as we went in our pairs, I could hear instructions being shouted. This enabled the remainder of the lads to know which room to take out next.

It was now organised chaos.

I couldn't hear a thing through the radio set and had no idea how the other two sections had fared. But the training team were present throughout the attack and intervened with advice when they saw fit. They also decided how many casualties we sustained during the fire fight. Eventually we cleared the fort and the firing died down. I gave a quick contact report over the radio and established the ammunition and casualty states for the section.

Once everything was back under control and the jetty had been secured, we waited a short while for the raiders to return. Clambering aboard, we were then whisked off to another location.

The next day, we carried out patrolling and map-reading tasks, without let-up. At the fall of darkness the troop moved towards a small beach, remaining tactical, after a section had moved forward to check for potential enemy.

Once we were assembled, we sent a radio message, and moments later ridged raiders arrived to pick us up. From the beach, we charged off to yet another new location. By now, I didn't have a clue where we were or where we were going.

Immediately getting soaked to the skin, the section was dropped off to commence another yomp! Corporal Locke was the only one in the section who knew where we were going.

It was now a test on how to keep going. The pace was intense and before long we all began to feel the strain. After a while we moved onto a disused railway line. The ground we were travelling across wasn't particularly hilly but the loose rocks, which had once been used as a base for the now missing track, were extremely hard under my feet. This was mainly due to the weight I was carrying, speed and the fact my boots were still wringing wet. Suffering with every step, I continued to push myself along.

John had also started to suffer. I could hear his moans as he lagged at the back of the section. He had been having slight problems with his feet at the start of the exercise, which weren't helped by the unbearable surface underfoot. It was now my chance to try and give him some encouragement; many weeks before on Hunters Moon he had helped to push me along.

'Come on, John, keep fucking pushing!'

'I am, I am, I am,' he moaned.

'Get back up the front of the section!'

'I'll try to!'

'Don't try, just fucking do it!'

With an extra bit of effort he pushed through the pain barrier and reeled in the distance between us.

'Now fucking stay there, you wimp!'

Compared to the start of training it now seemed to be automatic teamwork. Encouragement was always at hand. Corporal Locke continued moving forward and I began to wonder how far we were actually going to go.

During the night, we yomped for a number of hours along the railway line before returning to a tarmac road. I felt relief as I moved onto this surface. The morale-boosting feeling was short-lived, however, because the flat terrain of the railway line soon gave way to a steep uphill gradient.

My knees felt as if they were filling with water after each step. The soreness of blisters on my heels made me shudder to think what I was going to uncover when I eventually took my boots off.

Everybody in the section was digging out blind to stay with the pace of the yomp. Nobody wanted to fail and it was the thought of having to do it again that kept me going.

Eventually, as I reached the top of the hill, I spotted the RV point. One of the other sections was already there but they looked in a worse state than we did.

I took the opportunity to get a wet (mug of tea) whilst we waited for the rest of the troop. Sitting drinking my tea and thinking of my sore and swollen feet, I realised where the name 'Sea Sting' had come from.

A couple of casualties had been sustained through the march (injuries to legs and knees), but nobody dropped out from our section. I was then busy getting my feet and body sorted out in preparation for what was to come next.

After a short ride in the back of a Bedford truck it was well into the next day. We were given a short briefing, after which we moved to an LUP (lay up point).

The exercise progressed rapidly at this pace, with everything from patrols, NBC and ambushes being put to the test.

There were times when the troop started to falter in motivation. This was normally down to being exhausted but this wasn't allowed as an excuse. The training team also quickly rectified it, the normal punishment being a bout of 'shoot to kill'.

This meant that when the team saw fit, they instructed us to line up, hold our SLR at arm's length, and run around with locked-out elbows. Due to our run-down condition, this quickly became painful. It didn't take us long to realise that physically it was far easier to get the job done than be put through this punishment every time.

The week seemed to fly by and before long I found myself climbing aboard yet another raider. I cannot recall exactly where I went during the exercise other than most of it was spent on Dartmoor and south coast.

After a relentless week and racing under the Tamar Bridge in a rigid raider, I recognised we were in Plymouth Sound. The weather had turned very cold and daylight was giving way to darkness.

We were now on the final assault of the exercise, which indicated that end ex wasn't far away.

Like the opening operation of Sea Sting in Portland, the objective was a disued fort in Cornwall.

Moving to the assault start line seemed to be the easy part. The section task involved abseiling into a moat in order to take the lower rooms whilst the remainder of the building was attacked by the troop. Timing was the key to the operation's success, coupled with the thought of completing the exercise the next morning.

The abseil went according to plan and we were right on cue as the attack went in. As always, it was organised chaos. The extremely sore feet and tiredness which I had accumulated over the week vanished in an instant.

The objective had been taken by first light and, after our

initial reorganisation, the rumours around the troop were rife that end ex was going to be called. Again, my morale took another battering when we were instructed to get our bergens on and begin yomping.

The training team wanted to see how we reacted when told to start yomping when we were mentally prepared for end ex. The order was, 'Keep going until we tell you to stop!'

I was shattered, mentally drained and physically exhausted due to the pressure of the preceding weeks. But delving into my amazingly never-ending reserves, I kept going and continued with the troop down to an isolated cove.

Step by step I moved painfully towards the shoreline and soon noticed a number of raiders waiting. Then to my immense relief, the troop boss called end ex and the raiders took us on a journey to Stonehouse Barracks in Plymouth.

Once inside the warm confines we were given a short debrief on the overall exercise by the troop sergeant. I then ate the best breakfast imaginable, courtesy of the chefs in the galley, before setting off back to CTC. Temporarily, I forgot to ponder my overall performance as I climbed into my sleeping bag, sleeping solidly all the way back to CTC in the back of a four-tonner.

The remainder of the day was spent getting kit cleaned. In the middle of this, the troop sergeant called us onto the landing.

This was the moment at which we would learn how we had all fared on Sea Sting. A number of names were read out and told to go to the instructor's office. The rest of us, to my delight, were told that we had passed. A few other individuals were warned to pull their fingers out on the Commando tests or face the inevitable failure.

* * *

By now the troop contained approximately 25 of the original members. Our overall strength had been increased slightly due to receiving a number of back troopers. Recruits were normally back-trooped because of injury which had prevented them from completing all the Commando tests with their original troop.

These lads seemed to settle in very quickly and before long we had completed the three practice runs on the Endurance Course.

The test week had begun!

The Endurance Course test started at 06.00 hours, with a brisk four-mile walk up to the start on Woodbury Common. The PTI would be waiting at the start line with a set of scales ready to check the weight of our webbing wasn't below the stated 22 pounds. On top of the weight from my webbing, I also had the extra 11 pounds of my SLR.

Following the timed practice runs on the course, we were placed into teams of equivalent speed. The fastest three set off first, followed by the next three fastest and so on.

I was with the first team, owing to my satisfactory performances on the previous runs. In my team were two big lads called Crane and Kelly. Crane was a very tall and athletic lad who could run for ever at an astonishing pace. Kelly wasn't particularly fast but he was very strong and pushed himself and his large frame beyond belief. I was in a good team.

The morning of the test was fairly cold and misty. Sarcastically, the PTIs remarked, 'At least there isn't going to be a problem with heat exhaustion!'

The whistle blew and we raced off, knowing that the next team would be setting off a few minutes behind us. If they caught us, we would more than have likely failed.

The first two miles of the course consisted of a variety of

water filled tunnels, deep pools, streams, steep hills and rocky tracks.

After the first tunnel, I found myself wading through Peter's Pool. I didn't particularly relish this part of the course because the pool, which was about 40 feet in length, came up to my nose. In the middle of the pool I had to swim to avoid drowning. The icy water also sapped the energy whilst doubling the weight of the webbing.

Breaking from the water's grasp, I hauled myself out and realised that I was now starting to 'hang out' (become exhausted).

Not having time to think about my condition, I saw that I was standing in a sheep dip up to my waist in water. This particular obstacle was a concrete construction with a hole in the middle. The only problem with the hole was the fact it had a stream running through it. I went one side with Crane, while Kelly moved round to the other side. Speed was vital, so without even thinking I gasped a lungful of air and dived down into the murky hole. Crane assisted in pushing me through, with Kelly standing at the other side trying to pull me out. I staggered to my feet gasping for air and turned immediately to push Kelly through. He didn't need any encouragement because he was already on his way back. No sooner had he got through than he helped Crane return, and I pulled him back, lifting his face to the surface by the scruff of his neck.

It was now a process of getting through the rest of the obstacles. The last one was the indication that we could break up and run the remainder of the four miles back to CTC on our own.

Before starting the course, we had agreed to try to stay together so that we could push each other along the way. I cannot describe what the scenery around the first two miles of the course was like, as I had to concentrate so hard on pushing myself forward. The rocky paths were treacherous underfoot and it would have been easy to turn an ankle

I hit the tarmac road and began to run the four miles back to CTC along the twisty Devon roads. Now I was really suffering because I was racing against the clock. The water from all the tunnels had soaked me through to the skin and I began to feel the webbing biting into my back and hips. The water in my boots squelched with every step, causing the socks I was wearing to rub on my feet. Some kneepads that I was also wearing to protect myself in the tunnels against the razor-sharp rocks had slipped and started to rub around the tops of my boots. Putting the pain behind me, I pushed on towards CTC with Crane and Kelly.

Eventually we approached heartbreak lane, the last long stretch of road before reaching camp. I read the infamous sign that all Marine recruits of my era will remember: 'It's only pain, 500 yds to go!'

I was now very conscious of the time and was pushing myself as hard as possible. We were still together and our camaraderie raised my performance to the extent that we crossed the finish line in 68 minutes, four minutes within the time limit. I quickly gave the barrel of my SLR a pull-through with an oily piece of cloth, took ten rounds and inserted them into a magazine, then moved down to the 30-metre firing range.

Still slightly out of breath from my run, I started to fire the ten rounds at a small target within the exposures of the test. I had to hit the target at least six times out of ten. This wasn't normally a problem but because the weapon had been through so much shit, stoppages were common, which could result in failing for not getting enough rounds down the range.

Fortunately, I got all my rounds down and hit the target ten times!

I was now extremely pleased because I had passed the first test without any major problems. It also made me feel better knowing that Kelly and Crane had also passed the test. I left the range and started to walk back to the accommodation, shouting words of encouragement to a few lads just returning to the camp, and suddenly realised how shattered we all must have looked to anyone driving past.

At the end of the first day most of the troop had passed this test, other than a couple who had failed for being outside the time limit.

Early next morning we set off on the nine-mile speed march. This was done, as a troop, around the local area. We carried the standard equipment for all the tests: 22 pounds of webbing and our rifles, and we had to finish in 90 mintues.

This test seemed to be easier than the previous day because it involved staying with the pace of the troop. The only really uncomfortable periods were when we began to march up hills in quick time rather than run. This extra pressure on my shins caused immense pain in the muscles below my knees.

There was a tradition for the Company Commander to come on the speed march. He was an experienced officer in his late thirties and kept a reasonable distance from the troop throughout our training. I very rarely saw him around CTC. His physique, as one would expect from a man of his age, was slightly beer-bellied and a few pounds overweight. But to my surprise this made no difference to his very good performance on the nine-miler. He completed the test carrying the same amount of equipment as everyone else.

At the end of the march, we carried out a section attack where we had to fire and manoeuvre for a while.

Other than being out of breath for an hour and a half and sustaining yet sorer feet, I completed this test without any hiccups.

The OC then gave us a quick debrief and a few words of encouragement for the remainder of the tests.

To my surprise, the march had claimed a couple of failures. I wasn't shocked when I heard their names because I had learnt during training that a few characters in the troop had found it difficult when the going got tough. I am sure that this was due to their lack of determination when required to push themselves through the pain barrier.

The following morning, back at camp, I prepared for the Tarzan Assault Course. I took the opportunity to examine my injuries and administer first aid to myself, treating the various abrasions I had accumulated over the last two days. The worst of these were on my hips, where the constant running had caused the wet webbing to rub away the skin. I treated them with a good painful scrub of warm, clean water. Once the exposed flesh had dried, I sprayed it with a stinging iodine solution provided by the medics. I then dressed the sores with clean dressings and made sure they were secure for the next day's activity.

The next day, after a relatively peaceful evening, I awoke to the knowledge that I had yet another test in front of me.

The Tarzan Assault Course was conducted in the same manner as every other test. The fastest member of the troop set off first, followed in order of timings from the last practice run.

I was the third to go and, on reaching the top of the 80-foot death slide, I noticed how windy it was. But there was no time to admire the scenery before the clock began. I dropped from the top of the death slide and raced down the rope, hanging to a strop as I went. Due to the damp and wet condition of the rope, the descent was faster than usual. I was extremely glad of the brakeman at the bottom as I quickly approached the end of the rope and the wooden boards. Once I had stopped, I timed my drop from the obstacle in order to land squarely on my feet. This was essential because the weight of my kit affected the centre of gravity in my body. To overbalance and fall would almost certainly mean injury.

Dropping to my feet, I raced off towards the other obstacles. I pushed myself around the various high-wired walks and crawls like a possessed gymnast until I reached the balance beam.

This particular obstacle had been the downfall of many previous recruits. This was due to their bottling out on a jump across a gap into a cargo net on the other side. The balance beam itself was only about 15 feet above the ground, but whilst running across it seemed far higher.

Slamming my fears to the back of my mind again, I raced down the beam as fast as the wet conditions allowed. Gritting my teeth and holding my breath, I leapt across the chasm, punching my arm into the net. I bent my elbow immediately to prevent myself bouncing off. I had done it without any hesitation, and continued to pump my arms and legs until I reached the bottom obstacle.

It was now a case of putting the pain behind me and pushing one foot in front of the other around the edge of the camp towards the beginning of the assault course.

The run had caused the blood in my head to start thumping and a dry burning sensation had developed in my lungs as I gasped for air. The assault course was now very familiar to me and I knew that if I continued to push myself around, I was in with a good chance of passing the test.

I pumped every piece of energy from my body and suddenly found myself approaching the 30-foot wall. I knew that once I reached the top, the test and pain would cease. Clenching the rope with both hands, I began to haul up my exhausted body. Every step that I took was painful and I actually felt like stopping to cry. But I couldn't give up after all the hard work and effort I had put in.

Reaching the summit, I jumped over the top of the wall and shouted to the PTI with his stopwatch. 'Recruit Bywater, Corporal!'

'Well done, lad, eleven and a half minutes!'

I had passed well within the 13 minutes. I was delighted because this test had definitely hurt me the most.

After everyone had completed the test, it was discovered that a couple of lads who had failed the Endurance Course had also failed this test, so they were back-trooped in order to do the test week again. Thankfully, I wan't one of them!

All I had to do now was pass the 30-miler across Dartmoor.

Later that afternoon we were given a briefing on the 30-mile march. The troop sergeant told us what to expect. He explained where the check points would be and what the route involved.

The march would start at Okehampton Camp in North Dartmoor and we would make haste in a southerly direction, taking in various checkpoints as we went. I had the added responsibilities of leading the section and thus had to prepare a route card which contained the relevant bearings and timings for the march.

The checkpoints were designed not only for the safety aspect but they also enabled us to work out where we needed to be at various times, as it was a march against the clock.

After this briefing, the troop set off for Okehampton Battle Camp in the back of a four-ton truck. Before leaving, I ensured I had plenty of Mars Bars and chocolate for the next day and continued to get plenty of fluids down my neck. On reaching Okehampton Camp, I gorged on more food in an attempt to stockpile my energy reserves.

Later that evening, the troop medic paid us a visit to check everyone's feet and offer advice about strapping our bodies up for the yomp.

The next morning, I grabbed a quick breakfast and chatted about the yomp with the rest of the section. We all had our own ideas about it, like when to run, when to walk and what the pain was going to be like. Preparing myself mentally, I forced these fears to the back of my mind.

The troop was setting off in sections at 15-minute intervals from the back gate of Okehampton Camp. We were going second. An instructor would accompany each section on every leg of the march.

Collecting my kit, I took the opportunity to have a quick chat with Phil and Mick and wish them luck. We had become good friends due to the preceding weeks of hardship. It was still dark but on the verge of getting light when we moved to the rear of the camp.

The first section set off and advanced up the small winding road. My eyes followed them for a few minutes until they eventually disappeared out of sight into the great abyss of Dartmoor. By now the sky had lightened to reveal an overcast day with heavy cloud cover. The wind was gusty and it had started to drizzle.

Waiting patiently and ready to go, I thought back to a comment the OC of Chatham Company had made to us at the beginning of week 15: 'If it ain't raining, it ain't training!' Since that memorable day, it had rained on every exercise and every Commando test!

Receiving final words of encouragement, we set off up the slow climb to the moors. The first thing I tried to do was establish a good pace. We quick marched up all the major hills but ran across all the rest.

Before long, we moved from the tarmac road onto the moors, where I started to concentrate on my compass and map-reading skills. I had learned to put great faith in the prismatic compass I held and was very conscious of the scenery around me. I checked and re-checked between compass and the ground that we were travelling in accordance with the map and route card.

The terrain underfoot was typical British moorland, wet lumps of grass on a soft peat base that could easily turn an ankle. This was the main surface of the march and my feet soon became soaking wet. The pace of the march was also very important. If we started too fast it might mean that some of the section would suffer on the later stages, and if we were going too slowly it might mean a time gap that was impossible to make up.

After a couple of hours and the first checkpoint, the weather had started to clear, giving us sunny intervals between the heavy clouds. Everyone was doing fine and everything was going to plan. Whilst I was pounding along I began to feel proud of what I was doing. I realised that I only had to finish the march to prove to my family and friends that I did have what it took to get my Green Beret. I also felt that I was now becoming a member of a very elite and special family.

It was these thoughts that kept me pushing harder and harder to achieve my schoolboy ambition.

At the final checkpoint we were ahead of schedule by about 45 minutes. The Company OC was now with us, along with Corporal Locke, who had joined us at the final checkpoint. There was now only a few miles to go but my feet, like everybody else's, had began to suffer from the constant hammering they had received over the last few days. My toes felt as if they were swelling in my boots. This caused them to become as painful as if they had been burnt and bruised.

Ignoring the pain, I started to navigate up the final major climb of the march.

Ryder's Hill is one of the largest and highest features on Dartmoor, so it was now a real final effort to get over it. As I climbed, I began to get sharp pains down my back from leaning into the hill. Just as I thought I was getting to the top and giving words of encouragement to the lads, the hill flattened out and continued upwards. There must have been three or four false ridges on the hill and to say it was demoralising was an understatement. My body kept telling me to stop but my mind was so determined I just pushed and pushed through the pain.

Eventually we reached the summit and began the fast descent towards the finish. I climbed over a small gate near to the bottom of Ryder's Hill, and proceeded along a small unclassified road. I knew it was now only a matter of a few hundred metres until I reached the end of this ordeal, but I sensed everyone's concern as the clock rapidly ticked towards the eighth hour.

They began to ask me repeatedly, 'How far do we have to go?'

At this point, I really felt under pressure. I knew that if we failed to get in under the time, I would have to accept most of the blame.

Corporal Locke appeared to notice these concerns and gave me a few words of encouragement: 'Good effort. Don't start flapping; there are no problems.'

That was easy for him to say. I, on the other hand, was still obsessed with the time, continually checking my watch.

Suddenly, to everyone's relief, I raised a massive smile when I saw the Final RV point some 400 metres from where we were. The rush of emotion through my body was indescribable. I had earned my Green Beret! I was so happy all I wanted to do was congratulate my oppos. Immediately, I realised that only a limited number of people experience the emotions of completing the Commando tests and earning the Green Beret.

It had taken us 7 hours 45 minutes to complete the 30-miler, and in my opinion it had been the most demanding test. The first section had got back before us and were already getting themselves sorted out. I noticed how the atmosphere had changed. The instructors also appeared to have changed and talked and congratulated some of the lads.

After a short while the final section made it back within the eight-hour time limit. Everyone was very pleased with their performance and I took time to congratulate them. The troop boss and OC came over to praise us all before we returned to CTC.

It was on the journey back to CTC that I realised how much my feet had suffered over the last eight hours. My toes were swollen from the constant pressure and pounding they had been put through on the march.

I was glad it was all over. Tremendous relief combined with the extreme satisfaction at what I had achieved. We had been through a tough period in our lives and we had all changed because of it. It had been a hard learning process, which either makes or breaks. We had made it, and had a hidden confidence in how to undertake anything. I was fully conscious of my own capabilities, which I had learnt about the hard way, from punishment both physical and mental. I had high regard for everyone who had come through this with me. I had been stretched to the limit every day for 30 weeks and now my mental awareness was sharper and I was in good physical shape. I felt tough and now had nothing to prove to anyone.

Back at camp, I sorted myself out and after, getting something to eat, I hobbled over to the payphone to speak with my parents. I couldn't wait to tell them the news. They seemed delighted with my achievement and said they would be down to watch my passing-out parade.

The hard work had finished but I still had one week left at CTC. Now, 296 troop had become the Kings Squad, and I spent most of the final week preparing for the passing-out parade.

It was during week 30 when they told me where I was going to be drafted: 40 Commando RM, in Taunton. The unit itself had just begun to arrive back to the United Kingdom after a six-month tour of Belize.

The majority of lads in the troop also received drafts to 40 Commando, though a few of the unlucky ones found themselves being drafted to Commanchio Company in Scotland.

The passing-out parade quickly arrived and lots of families came down to watch us pass out as fully trained Marine Commandos. I felt extremely proud of my achievements as I marched onto the parade square in time with the Corps Band playing, 'A Life on the Ocean Wave'.

After being inspected by a high-ranking Admiral, I went to the camp's theatre to receive my Green Beret. This was what I had joined and worked so hard to earn. In the last 30 weeks I had grown up considerably and was at this time prepared to lay my life down for the Corps. Out of the original of the 44 lads with whom I had initially started training, 20 had successfully completed the course. With all the back troopers, 33 of us eventually received our Berets on this day.

At the conclusion of the formal events, I broke off to say hello to my parents and brothers, who had made the journey down from home.

Eventually it was time to leave. So I said my goodbyes to my mates and took time out to shake the hands of all the training team who had put me through hell and back over the course.

Dashing to my room in order to collect my kit, I noticed the troop photo on the wall outside the training team's office. It still contained all the faces of the original troop and those of who had been crossed off owing to failing for one reason or another. Thinking this would be a good souvenir in years to come, I ripped it from the wall and stuffed it into my jacket pocket.

I had a very big smile when I drove from the gates of CTC but yet felt sad that I would never see my close friends again.

5

LEARNING THE TRADE

After the excitement of passing out and a short weekend off I quickly returned to reality when I stepped from the train at Taunton railway station. I chose the easy option of taking a taxi to my new destination because of the large amount of kit I was carrying.

Norton Manor Camp was a 15-minute ride which took me through the outskirts of Taunton. As I sat in the taxi, the passing scenery seemed to vanish into insignificance as I pondered on what lay ahead. My life was about to take another change in direction.

Before making any kind of personal assessment of the new people about to enter my life, I decided I was going to keep quiet and establish who was who. I had developed the skill of keeping quiet and sizing people up whilst changing schools. From this I could identify people's strengths and weaknesses, especially when it came to trusting them.

Eventually the taxi drew to a halt outside the main gates of 40 Commando RM. Quickly paying the driver, I dropped my belongings onto the footpath. Anxiously, I studied my new home as the diesel engine of the taxi rattled in the background.

Once the noise had vanished I couldn't help noticing how quiet the place was. The only person I could see was a

Marine standing at the main gate holding an SLR, his face devoid of any kind of emotion.

Grabbing my kit, I walked towards the dreary-looking guardroom, showing my ID card as I went in. Inside, not knowing what was going to be said to me, I anxiously identified myself to the Corporal Guard Commander, giving my full name, rank and number.

Subconsciously I somehow expected a rollicking. I was just fresh from recruit-training, where corporals were feared.

So I got something of a shock when he replied, 'All right, mate, just bear with me and I'll find what company your going into.'

Life in a Commando unit was clearly going to be far more relaxed than the non-stop regime of CTCRM.

Whilst waiting to find out where I was going, I stepped outside to have another quick glance at the camp. It consisted mainly of single-storey wooden Nissen huts which had been built shortly after the war. Little refurbishment had been carried out since, so the living accommodation was fairly poor. From above, the huts looked like squashed cardboard spiders. They contained a central block for washing, with two main corridors that ran down either side. These interconnected six 60-foot by 20-foot accommodation rooms.

The grounds around the blocks were pleasant, located close to woodlands inside the perimeter fence. Of course, the officers' mess occupied the most scenic spot towards the far side of the camp, in what was probably the old manor house.

Eventually the Guard Commander came out and told me I was going into B Company. One of the Marines on duty escorted me to the temporary accommodation block, where

I was shown a bed for the night. Walking down the main road through the camp, I noticed there didn't seem to be a soul around. Because the unit had only just returned from a six-month tour of Belize, everyone was still on weekend leave.

In the accommodation area itself, I discovered how sparse the furniture was. The only obvious items were a few primitive iron beds and serviceable lockers.

Dumping my belongings into a locker I decided to walk over to the NAAFI bar in order to take a look around and grab something to eat. The place was empty. The only thing to do was watch TV.

This was it!

I felt suddenly as if the last 30 weeks had been wasted. My mind wandered, thinking about whether I would eventually meet someone I knew or if anybody would actually speak to me.

After an hour or two the bar area started to fill up with lads who had just returned from their weekend leave. Because of the lack of conversation I decided to go back to my room in order to get ready for the early start.

So, feeling somewhat out of place in my new environment, I was amazed to discover Mick and Phil unpacking their kit. I couldn't believe it; they had both been drafted into B Company! We spent the remainder of the night chatting about what we had all been up to over the leave period.

Come the morning and an early breakfast, I learned that I was joining 4 Section, 5 Troop. Mick was also joining the same troop but Phil found himself going elsewhere in the company.

The first day was spent doing my joining routine, visiting the various stores and admin offices to let them know I was now in the unit. I quickly discovered how relaxed everybody was, especially the corporals and sergeants.

Everyone had passed the Commando course and was expected and relied upon to carry out a job without letting the side down.

5 Troop, B Company was full of different characters ranging in age from late teens to middle twenties. The oldest member of my troop was Dave, who had joined the Corps rather late in life at 28.

The experience of talking, working and living with a wide cross-section of adult males helped me to mature very quickly. I rapidly settled into the routine of daily life in the unit, which varied considerably, depending on future trips and exercises.

The troop took every opportunity to get out of camp for the day. Regular trips to the nearby Quantocks proved popular. I learned to develop my map-reading skills with activities such as orienteering, always a highly competitive event in the company – the crate of beer for the winner probably being the main reason for this.

Another day was spent travelling to Minehead. The plan was to yomp most of the morning along the coast, finishing on the seafront itself.

We set off on a beautiful summer's morning. I quickly discovered that the pace wasn't particularly exerting. In the words of the troop boss, 'A chance to enjoy the scenery.'

Come the end of the 'Stroll', we finished on the beach close to the town.

As I wondered what was to happen next, somebody produced a baseball bat from a Bergen and we spent the remainder of the day playing baseball. This was great.

Whilst relaxing in the sunshine, it dawned on me that this was what life in a unit was all about: hard work followed by an opportunity to relax and get to know my new colleagues. All I needed now was the travel!

The Corps expected everyone to maintain his own physical fitness. You didn't have to be a superman. All they required was that the individual could cope with what was needed in the field. In other words, plenty of endurance. Every day the troop spent an hour or so doing phizz and, when time permitted, I tried to train on my own in the evenings. This was usually a short run or a sport of some kind.

I was now in the best possible physical shape of my life. Not only did this keep me healthy but it also increased my awareness and ability to keep my mind focused on a task over a long period of time.

Of course, it wasn't all work, train and work.

On most free evenings I soon got into the swing of a 'run ashore', going down town to indulge in the camaraderie of drinking as much alcohol as possible. The nights out never seemed to be in half measures. I don't think I ever went out and stayed sober in Taunton. Any excuse would do – birthdays, somebody's leaving do, or just a Thursday night before a weekend off.

At the time some might have frowned on our antics, but everything was meant to be harmless fun. Standing in a bar stark bollock-naked singing obscene songs with the rest of the troop was not unusual.

Now I realise that it was our way of letting off steam. Though we didn't think of it like that, it was how we reduced the stress levels created when working so closely together over a long period of time. These escapades also helped to develop a good morale, and when times got tough we could always draw a smile talking about what individuals had been up to (commonly referred to as 'performing').

97

Shortly after joining 40 Commando I started to notice increased media attention being paid to the subject of bullying within the Forces. There were occasions within my company when certain men were considered not to be pulling their weight. This was quickly identified and the punishment was normally carried out by shaving various parts of the offender's anatomy. If that person still didn't recognise that he had a problem, it would then be pointed out to him by one of the senior lads within his section.

In my whole time in the Corps I never came across any bullying. In my view it was another topic for journalists to create and blow out of total proportion.

Before long, I found myself travelling north for the unit exercise. The company had crammed itself onto two coaches and the drive to Otterburn seemed endless.

Eventually we broke from the grip of the motorway network to discover how delightful the scenery in the North of England is. The mountains and rolling hills looked like nothing I had seen before. Staring at them, I started to imagine that I was passing an art gallery. The only thing missing from these real-life oil paintings was the wooden frames.

Arriving at the transit camp, we were dropped off and I again noticed how sparse the accommodation was. Fortunately this was only going to be our stop-over point.

Later that night, after our evening meal, the troop boss gave his orders for the next day's operation.

The night passed quickly, owing to the early start, and before long I was in back-breaking pain as we moved as professionally as possible over the rugged countryside. The visions of oil paintings had rapidly vanished as I struggled with my Bergen and equipment.

I now discovered that the yomps in training were easy compared with this first experience of them in a unit. I began to wonder whether I would be able to keep up with the section if the pace and intensity were maintained for the remainder of the exercise. On the first day I questioned my ability but soon realised that it was just as hard for every-body else in the section. During this exercise I began to get closer with some of the others from the troop.

My oppo in the section and for the rest of the exercise was a big West Country lad called Carl. He had passed his Commando tests a few months before me and joined RM Poole, awaiting the return of the unit from Belize. Not much older than myself, he had a great sense of humour but could lose his temper when pushed. We got on great.

After a few days of being on the move and carrying out vari-ous patrols and section attacks, we were given the order to 'dig in'. The troop boss explained in his briefing that red forces (enemy) were now on the counter-offensive and the Company OC expected us to be in and concealed by first light.

This order couldn't have come at a worse time, as I felt completely shattered. However, the pain wasn't going to stop me because I was determined to show the rest of the lads how I could hack life in a Commando unit. I also wanted to give the impression that they could rely on me to get a job done. I really exerted my aching body to assist Carl in digging our two-man trench.

'OK,' I said, 'let's get cracking, and the sooner we're in, the sooner we can get our heads down!'

Carl gave me a blank expression and began laughing as we started to de-turf and dig down.

Did he know something that I didn't?

We had been specifically placed in a position within the section and troop location so that all the arcs of fire towards the approaching enemy could be covered. We were not allowed to move our trench.

After a few hours we had managed to dig down three feet when we heard the spade chink as it hit rock.

Could it be a large stone? I thought as the vibration from the wooden handle raced up my arm.

Chink, chink! Fuck me, I don't believe it! To our horror, we had struck solid rock. Now we were really going to be hard pushed to be in before first light.

The task became very slow going and my already aching back began to suffer even more. The only comfort that I could draw upon was that everyone else in the section was in the same predicament.

By morning we had just about completed our task but it had been at the expense of our hands and backs. Most of my fingers had blisters in various shapes and formations. The pain from standing upright felt as if a red-hot poker had been slapped across my back.

I was now very tired and I only had a short while to prepare something to eat before the first attack came in.

Recce troop had adopted the role of red forces so, needless to say, we were 'stood to' for the remainder of the day. It was now about four days into the exercise and I still hadn't had any sleep worth the mentioning.

Not only was I shattered from the lack of sleep, I had also discovered that midges plagued Otterburn at this time of the year and thoroughly enjoyed eating me.

On the morning of the second day in the trench our routine was slightly interrupted when we had an unexpected visitor. He was very fast and more than adequate at spending long periods of time out on the hills. Where he came from nobody knew. However, for the remainder of the day the black and white sheepdog became our faithful companion. I put it down to the amount of bacon grill he ate rather than his liking for us. But he was worth it because he brought a smile to our faces.

The three days we spent dug in were extremely uncomfortable owing to sleep deprivation and weather.

On the final night of the exercise the bosses planned our withdrawal from the trench in order to reorganise for the unit night attack.

The move to our designated start line went according to plan but became uncomfortably cold as we waited for the signal to move off.

Once this time signal arrived, chaos developed as everyone began firing and charging towards their targets. The noise was deafening, with various battle Sims [simulations] exploding nearby. I had no idea what orders were being shouted, but the training and teamwork gave me some kind of clue as to what I should have been doing. Eventually we fought our way through the mock enemy position to reorganise. I shuddered to think how many casualties we would have received if we had been doing it for real.

Thankfully, though, come first light end ex was called. I had survived my first unit exercise but it hadn't been without a fair amount of pain.

From this point we moved back to the transit camp, where I cleaned myself up and stepped aboard the coach back to Taunton. Sleep was instant!

40 Commando RM was known as 'the sunshine unit' within the Corps because they generally got all the trips to the sunny countries. Before having any time to settle back into

life at sunny Norton Manor Camp I found myself setting off for an amphibious Nato exercise.

Fortunately, due to the lack of amphibious ships owned by the government, I found myself embarking onto a civilian ferry. The comfort of a four-man cabin was a bit nicer than my accommodation block in Taunton. I also found that I was sharing a room with Mike.

The other two lads sharing the room with us were called Scouse McGrath and Buster Brown.

Scouse became a very good friend of mine and a close run ashore oppo. He was heavily into boxing and was a person who could drink for England and still get out of his bed and put in remarkable running times with the troop.

Buster was very different. He never did any self-motivated physical training and constantly had a fag in his mouth. He always pleaded poverty and constantly borrowed money towards the end of the month.

Shortly after setting sail, I quickly settled into the ship's routine. The upper deck was allocated for an hour to each troop, so that we could keep up our fitness over the coming weeks.

Whilst the day-to-day life on board continued for ourselves, the Navy carried out training procedures with the other Nato ships from the armada. Every now and then the ship turned hard to port or starboard. I later found out that it was supposed to be an anti-submarine manoeuvre. Unfortunately, I kept thinking about the Falklands and the sinking of the *Belgrano*. I naturally assumed that if a submarine wanted to attack us it wouldn't have had much problem hitting our bright white ferry!

The exercise had been named 'Bold Fox – Blue Guard', and the main landings were to take place in southern Norway close to the town of Larvik.

It was now into autumn, which meant at least we were going to miss the winter weather.

Eventually, after travelling around the north of Scotland and taking in some beautiful scenery, the troop began to prepare for the forthcoming landings. The briefing explained how we were going to muster at our disembarkation points in order to climb down the rope nets into the awaiting LCVPs. Once ready, we were going to land at an isolated beach that should have already been secured by another company. We would then move through their positions and advance to contact.

The new troop sergeant was a PTI by qualification and had a good sense of humour, which in turn had a good effect on us.

Again everything was carried out with a hundred per cent professionalism. The landing went according to plan and I managed to stay completely dry. The weather was also sunny, so in all I couldn't complain about anything.

The troop's aim for the exercise was to improve section drills and tactics. The Norwegian Army played the enemy and this rivalry also increased professionalism, especially when patrolling. No one wanted to get caught out.

On the large Nato exercises we also had Directing Staff to assess the reality of the operation and keep control. During some of the attacks they would identify people who had been injured and to what degree. It was very easy for company commanders and troop officers to overlook this potential nightmare whilst training, but it was extremely important to consider casualties, not only from the humanitarian point of view and the subsequent effects on morale, but it could also affect the momentum of an attack if too many people stopped to tend the injured. Now, problems were caused by the extra men needed to treat casualties.

After the first day of this exercise I quickly found that the temperature took a tremendous turn for the worse once the sun had begun to dwindle in the sky. It became very cold at night and the extra clothing from my Bergen was a great help.

Early the next morning we prepared for a troop assault. Our SOP (standard operational procedure) was to drop our Bergens at a pre-located position in order to collect them after the assault. In my view, this was a slap-dash approach. It highlighted the fact that frequent training can sometimes ignore the possibility of the unexpected in contacts with the enemy. It was always anticipated that once the objective had been taken we would go and collect our Bergens. Alas, war isn't always like this and some battles last for hours, days and sometimes weeks, proving that Bergens and supplies cannot always be collected as planned.

What happened next, though, changed my whole attitude towards the equipment that I carried with me whilst working in the field.

The adrenaline was soon pumping its way around my body as I took up various firing positions once the assault had started. I soon forgot how wet and cold I was as I concentrated on finding the best cover from which to return fire.

The assault on the small village concluded fairly rapidly even though an hour or two had passed by. At this, point when we were reorganising ourselves, the DS staff explained that there had been a counter-attack and that our presence was needed elsewhere.

Thus we didn't have time to collect our Bergens and off we went. The boss told me that they would probably chopper them up to us later that day, and I believed him.

Oh, how I learnt from my naïve mistakes! I spent the next two nights freezing with the rest of the lads. It got so bad at times that I huddled together with my oppos in order to try and reap some heat from their bodies. The minutes ticked by like hours. It brought back the horrible feelings from my survival exercise in training.

The first question I always asked myself was, What the hell am I doing here? Hundreds of similar thoughts raced through my mind like, Why am I doing this when I could be at home in a nice warm house? It isn't as if I'm getting huge amounts of money. Could I really do this for the next 22 years?

I had no answers. From my own experience, there was no clear-cut reason for people joining the Marines and putting up with the harsh realities of living and working in extreme conditions.

As the night ticked by I again realised how resistant my body was to inclement weather. On this occasion I thought I came very close to getting hypothermia!

Thankfully after these two inhospitable nights we eventually received our bergens and set off for the next objective, a small cast-iron bridge in the middle of nowhere.

We were playing the enemy and our role was to hold this bridge whilst the Army Commando Engineers placed dummy charges over it. Not long after the Engineers had completed their task we found ourselves involved in another contact, with the Norwegians from across the other side of the river. Some of the lads were slightly pissed off owing to the early arrival of the 'Fish Heads' (Norwegians), which prevented us from getting any sleep. So, to seek some kind of revenge we removed the parachutes from the night illumination flares we had been carrying.

One by one red-hot lumps of phosphorous started racing over the river towards the Norwegians. I found this highly amusing. Oblivious to the potential dangers it caused, everybody in the troop roared with laughter as the Norwegians began to realise the danger. Then the DS staff started screaming their heads off.

The mock battle was subsequently won and we took the opportunity to get some sleep in between sentry duties.

The next day started with a tongue-in-cheek rollicking from the troop OC. He had received a lecture from his superiors after the Norwegians had complained to the DS staff about our skirmish the previous day. Of course, we were all well aware of the dangers but they seemed to forget it was a way of venting our anger after 'graving it' for two days with no supplies. ('Graving it' refers to Marines' front line work.)

The remainder of the day was spent getting as much forced rest as possible. A warning order had been given for an operation later that night. Forced rest wasn't particularly hard because the whole troop was shattered. I rapidly realised that on major exercises there were long periods of sitting around in harbour positions whilst the hierarchy played at their war games, using us as the pieces!

On my arrival I had noticed how clean and tidy Norway was. There never appeared to be any scruffy-looking houses, traces of rubbish or dog dirt on the pavements. Everywhere outside the main towns was covered in acres and acres of thick evergreen forest, which helped give that fresh and healthy appearance.

That evening I had the opportunity to observe one of the many beautiful sunsets in Norway. As I watched the sun disappear behind the horizon, the mountains, covered in thick blankets of trees, were transformed before my very eyes. Within seconds the trees changed from dull browns to highly-polished copper as the sun ebbed, and the surface of the mountains began to alter in shape and texture as the light crept away with the vanishing sun. Watching this and taking it all for granted, I again began to daydream of home.

Miserably, though, I was soon brought back to reality when the order to move was given. By now all our weapons had been checked and we set off for the next objective.

The overall plan for the company was to take and occupy a small town close to another main road bridge. Our own objective was to fight through and capture the town, assisted by a second troop from the company. Whilst we did this the third troop would take a bridge on the outskirts of the town, supported by American Cobra gunships.

The start line for the assault was at the edge of a cornfield at the town's borders. When we were in position, it began to rain heavily. When the order to move finally came, I was relieved to get going as I had started to get very cold. The field drenched me within seconds, but it didn't bother me in the slightest. I was now too busy concentrating on the objective of clearing the town.

At the edge of town, I noticed that there were a large number of outhouses and barns. The Norwegian Army would have probably had the life of Reilly awaiting our arrival. Just being dry and warm and out of the elements was a great boost for morale when in the field.

Everybody took the assault completely seriously, throwing thunder flashes and screaming out potential targets as we moved through the various buildings and gardens. The commotion was organised as everybody knew what to do. Our drills and training soon came together, even if it was a little confused.

After what only seemed like seconds, the town was cleared and I found myself on the edge of yet another field

107

by a pig farm. I sat here with the rest of the section waiting and waiting for a so-called counter-attack by the Norwegians. It never came!

Eventually down the chain of command somebody decided that we should get some sort of harbour routine going. I was now in a bad state, having sat in a fire position for four hours while freezing to death. Forcing myself to my feet, I suddenly noticed that my wet denims had frozen like cardboard around my legs. I was shaking violently and I realised how cold I was. I had to get a 'hot wet' into my system before I perished.

Motivating myself enough to search my saturated webbing, I clumsily lit my portable gas stove. The water from the bottle on my webbing seemed to take for ever to boil as it was so cold.

Eventually the water was hot enough to submerge a couple of tatty-looking tea bags. Once the water had changed colour I quickly began to consume it, gaining strength from each mouthful. These were some of the basic hardships of soldiering.

During the next two days, spent harboured up at the pig farm carrying out various patrols around the surrounding countryside, I experienced two rather rare events.

Whilst guarding the main road bridge one night with the section, I became aware that a company of Dutch Marines were working closely to our flank. On this particular night they should have replaced us at the bridge, taking over our responsibilities while we moved elsewhere.

It didn't materialise, owing to the fact that they had decided to go on strike! This was allegedly because of being pushed too hard during the exercise and not having enough sleep. Little did I know the Dutch Marines even had unions to represent them.

This may have been a marvellous peacetime strategy for the men, but what use would it have been during a conflict? It also didn't solve our problem at the time, as we had to stay freezing on the bridge.

The other rare experience that I came across was rather amusing to the troop.

Back at the pig farm, Mick had plumped for the 01.00 hours to 03.00 hours guard duty. Fortunately for him, he had the sentry position that overlooked the town. As this was a small community, day-to-day life for the locals was interrupted by our presence in the town, and a number of local girls soon began to stop and chat as they passed.

It wasn't long before Mick had struck up a rapport with one of these girls whilst doing his turn on the gun position. Like all true gentlemen he asked her back to his place. She readily accepted. Not bad going!

The only problem was that his place consisted of a dirty green sleeping bag located within a few feet of smelly saddleback pigs. His appearance also left something to be desired, since he had been in the field for the best part of a week.

Come the morning, Mick was the troop hero and rumours were running wild. He also seemed to be the happiest bloke on the exercise.

Soon we were re-embarking on ship and setting sail for the port of Alborg, in Denmark.

By the time we reached our destination my kit was ready for the next exercise and I was looking forward to my first-ever foreign run ashore.

During the day I became involved in the unit football team so I managed to occupy my time playing various Danish Army units. The hospitality was great but the results were somewhat up and down, mainly because of the hangovers everyone seemed to have.

At night I decided to take it easy whilst out with the lads in order to avoid any extra hassle that might have been caused by getting noticed. This didn't stop me from enjoying myself and I quickly learned the art of drinking vast amounts of bottled Elephant beer.

Scuffles and the odd fight sometimes broke out with the locals and when the local police became involved this normally resulted in a British Marine getting thrashed by them. Most altercations were quickly resolved, but if an incident did filter back to the ship the OC or RSM would normally have the last say.

Other than the football pitches and clubs I didn't see a great deal more of Denmark.

Back on board, we set sail in the general direction of the northern coast of Germany. The daily routine continued and I learnt more about the Soviet threat that existed at that time. Target recognition of a potential enemy was very important. Prior to joining I didn't have a clue what a T72 or T80 tank looked like, let alone their capabilities.

It didn't take long for the sea journey to start to drag slightly. Thus anything that amused us was a bonus.

Most of the entertainment took place in the bar playing cards and Trivial Pursuit, and general piss-taking. Most of us normally congregated together in the evenings, drinking as a troop as it was impossible to get to know everyone from the various companies on board.

*   *   *

During my short period with the troop I had got to know the six other lads from my section.

Charlie, the section commander, was one of the few coloured lads in the Corps at the time. I had recognised him from my time at CTCRM as he had rejoined while I was there. He had served with 40 Commando during the Falklands conflict but decided to leave the Corps when the hostilities had finished. He later told me that this was due to the influence of his girlfriend at the time. Unfortunately, once he had made the plunge to Civvy Street, she decided to leave him. Struggling to settle in the real world, he moved from one dead-end job to the next. He soon missed the camaraderie of the Corps and signed back on again after two years.

Back in the unit, Charlie was extremely keen to do well and get promotion. He was a great athlete, totally reliable and very professional in the field.

Dinger was an ex-Army signaller who had decided on a change in direction. He was a tall, daft lad who seemed to fall in and out of lust overnight. Dinger could be extremely fiery if wound up the wrong way, especially when he had consumed a few pints. This temper had got him into trouble during training when he decided to smack his drill instructor. This obviously wasn't a good move, because it resulted in him being sent to the Military Prison in Colchester to cool down for a while.

He was of Australian descent and was always talking about his ambition to get in the Aussie Army. He was fairly quiet and more intelligent than some of the lads gave him credit for. His mother lived in Luton so he quickly became a friend of mine, and the pair of us spent many days on leave getting pissed together.

Scouse McGrath was a true Scouser, coming from the

111

Anfield area of Liverpool. Somewhat surprisingly, he didn't seem to have any particular interest in football. He had a bubbly personality and I quickly grew to like him. When he had a pint down his neck he would try to shag any female. He also had a wicked sense of humour and was often amusing when he came to tell us about his exploits the next day. When it came to work, Scouse was extremely professional and had the ability to go on for ever during physical exertion.

Brian was a nice enough lad from Bristol. Unfortunately, when he did manage to get a word in amongst the others it was normally a load of bullshit. He seemed to have the uncanny knack of talking absolute nonsense without realising it. The Black Cat, as he was sometimes referred to, had done everything and anything better than anybody else had. I sometimes felt sorry for him because he did bear the brunt of the piss-taking but it was normally of his own making.

Nobby, a West Country boy, was probably the most academically qualified within the section. He was rather self-confident and a bit of a know-it-all. He had attempted to join the Corps as an officer. I found him rather cocky and instantly took a dislike to him. He had never given me any reason, but I felt I couldn't trust him, especially if it came to having our backs against the wall.

Finally there was Carl, who I knew was great, having worked with him in the field for so long.

Eventually we arrived near to the shores of Germany. The section was fully kitted and ready to go. I had made the final adjustments to my camouflage and equipment. It was now in the early hours of the morning and completely dark out-

112

side. None of the ship's external lights were on as we were now tactical. Everything had to be carried out in darkness or under an eye-straining red light.

We set off in line down one of the many corridors until we reached a store point. Here, lads from Mortar Troop were handing out mortar round cases. These were extremely heavy and weighed somewhere in the region of 20 pounds. Of course they didn't contain live rounds, but the sand inside gave us the opportunity to feel what it was like to take extra kit ashore on landings.

Strapping the case to the top of my Bergen, I attempted to pick it up. Eventually, after some help from the lads I managed to get the Bergen, which was now easily in excess of 100 pounds, on to my back. Stumbling to the disembarkation point, I awaited my turn to climb over the side of the ship and down the netting.

This was easier said than done.

Briefly looking down, I saw the LCU bobbing about some 30 feet below. The only thought racing through my mind at the time was, If I let go, I will fall between the ship and LCU and never be seen again!

The weather was cold, wet and windy, which didn't help matters. It took all the strength in my arms to reach the safety of the landing craft.

Once inside the LCU and under the cover of its roof, we were slowly crammed in like sardines. Nobody spoke as we travelled towards the shore and I took the opportunity to snatch a few minutes' sleep.

Two leg-cramping hours later I got the word to prepare to beach. The engines strained and the sound of sand scratching the underside of the craft could be heard.

The front ramp crashed down and I charged off into the knee-deep surf. The sea was bitterly cold but I tried to ignore this as I waded to the beach with the lads. Walking across the beach, I was handed a piece of orange tape to wrap around my arm.

We were now playing the enemy to the local British and German Army units.

As in all exercises, we set off yomping to a so-called harbour position in order to establish what would be happening next. The yomping was extreme. The straps of my Bergen felt as if they were trying to rip the shoulder blades from my back. The extra weight from the mortar case was also taking its toll. It became painful to remain and look alert. My arms began to suffer owing to the nerves in my shoulders hurting so much. This in turn caused pains and spasms to run down both of my arms. I soon found it difficult to hold my SLR in the correct patrol position across my chest. I was crumbling fast!

I quickly passed the pain barrier but for a horrible moment I thought about rapping. My personal pride was having an immense battle with my will to keep going.

Surely everyone else was suffering like me?

Then to my relief we reached a drop-off point for the mortar cases. I quickly threw my Bergen to the floor and ripped the case from it. By fuck, was I glad to see the back of that!

The break was just long enough to get my kit sorted out. Putting my Bergen back on, I quickly noticed the difference in weight and had no other problems for the remainder of the yomp.

The rain was constant but during the day I got involved in a few skirmishes with a number of German tanks. They were very intimidating on the battlefield, especially to us on the ground. I found their fire power, manoeuvring skills and daunting presence somewhat frightening but I still preferred to be on my own two legs than stuck in a potential ready-made oven!

Eventually, after being on the go for more than 24 hours, the section moved into a harbour position. From here we carried out patrol tasks for the next few days, which included attacking enemy positions.

The background and planning of a patrol depended greatly on the type of result you wanted from it. A basic clearing patrol around a new harbour area, for example, could be done fairly quickly; however, a recce patrol took lots of organising.

The skill of issuing a good set of orders could only improve with practice and was always done in an organised sequence. This included the type of ground to be covered, the situation regarding enemy activities, the aim of the mission and how it was to be executed. It also covered any supporting elements such as extra weapons, or what to do if prisoners were captured and finally, who was in command should there be any problems during the task. These points were individually broken down to cover finer aspects of the overall plan. Once the issuing NCO or officer had completed this, everyone was encouraged to ask questions so that any potential problems could be addressed. It was thought highly unprofessional to be sorting out a dilemma in the middle of a patrol.

I enjoyed the patrolling aspect because it was all about getting it right as a team. I also got a huge amount of satisfaction when we achieved the aim and everything went according to plan.

* * *

Then, as in all the exercises, we were given the order to dig in! This time I was sharing a trench with Buster. Fortunately, we managed to get the loan of a tractor, which assisted no end in the building of a massive trench. We used the time we had saved to get some well-earned rest.

I awoke to discover that my eyes were extremely sore because of the dusty confines of the trench. Sand and grit had got everywhere, making me most uncomfortable.

Sitting in the trench, dwelling on this fact, I began to feel cold and sorry for myself. But to my surprise one of the lads came over and told me to get myself sorted out in order to go out on patrol. I was delighted; I hated the fucking trench. The thought of stretching my legs and getting warm was better.

Quickly preparing my kit, I set off to a nearby field, joining other lads from the company. We had jointly formed another fighting troop in order to take part in a heliborne assault.

The scale of the planned attack quickly became apparent from the massive number of helicopters involved. I counted at least 40 Huey, Lynx, Sea King, Wessex and Sea Stallion helicopters. They were covering all the adjacent fields to the one I was crouched in.

After a short break I soon found myself clambering aboard a German Sea Stallion. Inside, I was amazed by its size and carrying capability.

Once seated and stretching my neck to a nearby window, I managed to watch the whole flight take off together. From my vantage point I couldn't help feeling indestructible. No enemy could possibly compete against a force like this! Glancing out into the adjacent air space, I felt as if I was on the set of a war movie. The pilot's skills were impressive, decisive and extremely professional.

The flight was low-level and breathtaking. The pilot moved our Sea Stallion extremely close to the ground, hugging the contours as he went. In places we couldn't have been more than 15 to 20 feet up.

All I knew was that we were going to get involved in a contact as soon as we landed.

As the wheels or our helicopter slammed to the ground, the back door swung open, revealing bright rays of sunshine. Seeing this, accompanied by a thumb-up from the crew, I automatically charged off the aircraft.

There was total chaos at first as we entered into the middle of firefight. But thanks to the element of speed and good luck, we quickly gained the advantage and wreaked havoc amongst their re-echelon units.

Our opponents were Americans and we soon had the unexpected problems of dealing with them as prisoners.

Everything was taken extremely seriously and this seemed to shock our detainees, especially when they were thrown to the floor and told to shut the fuck up! Some were very surprised when they had their weapons taken from them. I think it made them feel very vulnerable without their protection.

I rapidly began to realise that this operation was extremely far-fetched and if it had been for real a lot of us would have been going home in body bags.

Not for the first time did I feel slightly dubious about the way some senior officers planned assaults. I just hoped and prayed to myself that they would never consider direct heliborne assaults an option. In my view, they were potentially disastrous in any theatre of war, especially when the enemy was nearby.

But from a political point of view, this was a way in which the Top Brass used the military to impress the media, the politicians and ultimately the taxpayers.

By the end of the day I was starving and hadn't eaten for nearly 30 hours. Anything tasted good; even the brown biscuits from my 24-hour ration pack tasted like real Mcvities digestives.

Amazingly, once the operation had concluded, the choppers returned and took us back to the trench positions. I had half-expected to start a walk back to my trench.

Early next morning, after another uneventful night of being cold and miserable, I noticed a captain from the Fusiliers. Judging from his white armband and the way he was stumbling around, I assumed he was an exercise co-ordinator. I watched him visit all the trench positions, until he eventually reached Buster and myself.

As soon as he opened his mouth I took an instant dislike to him. With his public schoolboy accent he informed us that we were going to be attacked sometime today.

'About time,' I said.

He then told us in a patronising manner that, however unrealistic it seemed, we were going to be overrun and lose peacefully with no hand fighting!

The word lose wasn't in the Corps vocabulary book. There was no way that all the lads in the company would let some Pongo (Army) unit overrun our location.

As he turned and walked away, Buster picked up his spade and smiled. This might have been the officer's plan, but it certainly wasn't ours.

The excitement was short-lived because no one arrived to attack us, having allegedly got lost. End ex was called.

* * *

Another yomp. Mountain training in the Lake District 1990

Skiing in Norway 1989

Live firing on Dartmoor

30 weeks training and the
Kings Squad 1985

The Royal Marines Dog Section - Stonehouse barracks

Digging in on a feature in the Oman 1986

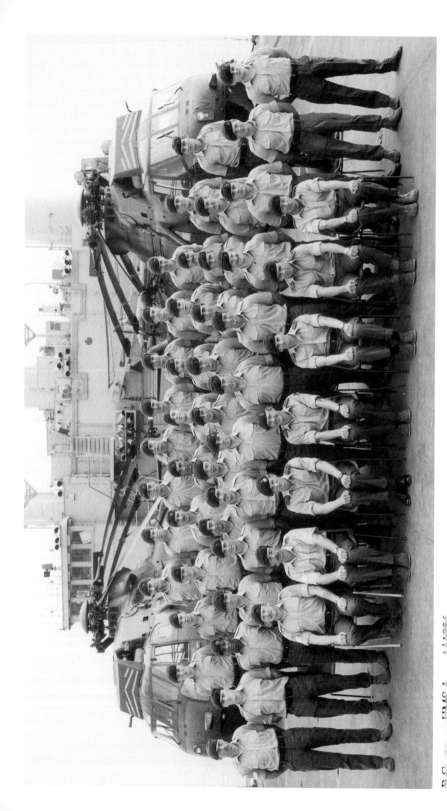

Egypt - 1986

The friendly Kurdish children

Batufa Iraq, 1991

Iraqi/Kurdish children returning home

A run ashore in Plymouth

The Cold War was still in full swing, so our training at the time was geared to deal with the Soviet threat. The Warsaw Pact, like Nato, closely monitored the build-up of troops in its bordering countries. As the Warsaw Pact classed Marines as storm troopers, they wouldn't have warmed to our presence in Germany. In fact, they would have considered us a potential threat to the East, and we could easily have caused a political problem if our presence had become public.

Hence our removal from Germany was rather unusual.

I was quickly instructed to collect my gear, wash in a tub of water and attempt to make myself look half-respectable. Then the troop boarded a local bus, which collected us from the edge of our isolated field. Once on board, we drove straight to Hamburg Airport and went through customs and onto a waiting Virgin 747.

The air stewardesses looked somewhat disgusted by our arrival. The smell of 200 bootnecks straight out of the field must have been overpowering to their delicate noses. But this didn't seem to matter because the main aim was to get us out of Germany with no fuss.

After a short flight, it was great to be back in the UK. The next day I was soon back into the swing at Norton Manor Camp and looking forward to 'getting up the line' on leave.

Most of the time I used travel warrants to get home but on some occasions Dave gave me a lift to the outskirts of London, where I would catch a train. Thumbing a lift was popular when I first joined, but as the terrorist threats increased we all stopped doing this.

Leave was nearly always a bit of an anti-climax. I loved going home to see my family but this only occupied so much of the day, especially when everyone else was at work.

During my time at home I would travel to Luton, where Dinger and I would spend our time getting pissed and performing in local bars. We even took to going out in fancy dress in the middle of the day. We never had anything to celebrate but it seemed to be entertaining, especially when most of the local population was at work. Some people found our antics highly amusing but others turned their noses up at us, probably thinking that we were lazy unemployed layabouts sponging off the state whilst they had to work. Little did they know who and what we were!

One night, whilst waiting for a taxi, Dinger and I spent half an hour boring the pants off a local bobby. He seemed to see the funny side of it as I tried to put the world to rights wearing nothing but a pair of fishnet stockings and French knickers.

The excitement and pressure release of leave quickly passed and I was soon back on the two-hour coach journey to Plymouth.

Arriving at Millbay Docks, I clambered aboard the awaiting LCU. Once it had been loaded to capacity, the vessel slowly crept into Plymouth Sound. I could clearly see the floating structure of HMS *Intrepid* drawing nearer and nearer.

I couldn't believe I was getting the chance to go aboard this famous Commando assault ship. A few years earlier her sister ship, HMS *Fearless*, had demonstrated how vital she was during the Falklands campaign.

HMS *Intrepid* was now going to be my home for the coming months, with our final destination being Oman in the Middle East.

Pulling alongside the warship, I realised how inventive someone had been to design a ship of this nature. The stern of the vessel was submerged into the sea, allowing the various landing craft to manoeuvre freely in and out of its own mobile port. The extra weight of water in the rear of the ship also caused it to list back, raising the bow upwards.

Once on board, having clambered through the various hatchways and metal stairways with fully-laden Bergens, we received a briefing in the galley area. It was a short introduction to living and working aboard a naval ship.

We were told when and where not to enter colour co-ordinated hatches around the ship. There were strict timings about when we were allowed onto the rear flight deck to undertake physical training and, more important, how mealtimes were to be arranged. Owing to the large number of Marines embarked and the naval ratings from the ship's company, meal times were to be organised into specific shifts. (This soon became hell, especially when the weather was rough. If our troop was the last to eat, the floor would be treacherous underfoot from all the previously spilt food.)

After the briefing, I was led with most of the troop to our new mess deck, 4L1. Reaching the bottom of the metal stairways, I was shocked to discover how cramped the conditions were going to be for the next few months. There were 21 of us, with all our kit.

The walls and ceiling to the mess deck were covered in an array of pipes, and down each side was a row of beds split into three levels. Parallel with these beds down the middle of the mess was the smallest set of lockers I'd ever seen. At first glance they appeared to be smaller than the ones at my local swimming pool. Placing my shirt, a pair of denims and washing gear into a locker, I discovered it could hold nothing else of any substantial size.

It soon became obvious that any time I wanted to move or get something from elsewhere in the mess, I had either to ask or wait for somebody to get out of the way. Patience was going to be tested!

Once I had sorted myself out I took the opportunity to go on deck and watch the vanishing coastline of England.

Time passed spasmodically whilst on ship but I soon realised how uncomfortable it could become. I had been warned the ship would enter the notorious Bay of Biscay during the night but I had taken little notice. While I was fast asleep in my bunk, the weather took a turn for the worst and I found myself being thrown about. I had to use the straps on my bed to fasten myself down to prevent falling out. The sound of waves crashing against the ship made it seem as if I was trying to sleep in a submerged freight container. This was aggravated by the fact that the mess deck was just below the water line. Lying there listening to the water, I began to imagine the chaos if the ship rolled too far to one side and turned turtle. How vulnerable I was to the cruel sea outside. I remembered watching the film, *The Poseidon Adventure* and began to imagine how I would make my own escape.

In the midst of this there seemed to be a trail of lads dashing to the heads in order to throw up. This seemed to make me feel worse, even though I didn't feel sick myself.

I remained awake all night being rhythmically thrown from side to side. God, I hoped I would soon get accustomed to this and develop my sea legs.

Of course, the cramped conditions didn't apply to everyone and the officers had much more space.

I found it hard to accept that we had such a strong class

system in our country. I was from a hard-working family and had been brought up to learn, share and respect other people as being equal. This wasn't the case, and I soon began to feel like a prisoner in these very cramped conditions.

Officers were not allowed to socialise with the men. This had been a tradition in the Forces from the very beginning and repeated through generations. I thought this rather old-fashioned. The officers seemed to think they were from another society, yet if I were at home carrying out another kind of job it would be perfectly acceptable to speak to and socialise with them. I hated the divisive class system, especially as the WWII Commando Memorial at Spean Bridge is inscribed with the words 'United we Conquer'.

I soon realised that the naval officers were far more pompous and arrogant than the Marine officers. This was probably on account of our harder and more testing recruitment procedure.

Before long we entered the Port of Gibraltar. It was symbolic for us to be visiting 'Gib' because the Corps had received one of its many battle honours. We were also going to be present on the Corps Birthday, which meant an excuse for a double piss-up.

As always, it was every man for himself once shore leave had been granted. I spent most of the time eating and getting drunk, only to be sobered up with a race up the Rock.

The view from the top was breathtaking. The surroundings below looked like miniature models. It soon became apparent how high we were when I saw the size of *Intrepid*.

Our short stay in Gibraltar quickly finished and we were soon back on the ship.

Routines on board ship continued as we sailed towards Cyprus. I was becoming used to the food in the ship's galley. Whilst queuing for my evening meal I normally took the opportunity to check the ships progress and direction from a chart on the wall. Reading the chart was far easier than planning it. It was very easy to sit back and expect to reach somewhere, but subconsciously I was glad of the Navy's skills.

The lads on the mess deck generally got on well with each other, but every now and then a scuffle would break out when tempers reached boiling point. They were normally resolved in seconds and were always over something trivial like what channel or video to watch on the ship's TV.

I spent many hours listening to music in the evenings on my bunk. I also started to enjoy reading, something I had hated as a child. One particular book that I read, based on a soldier's own account of active service, played a major influence in my desire to write this book.

When it came to leisure time, the Navy allowed us to have two small cans of beer everyday. On occasions we tried to save our cans up over the week so that a small party could be thrown. This had a major risk involved because if the matlos found any extra beer during rounds, we risked having it confiscated. The problem of storing crates of beer on the mess deck also became a problem.

During this phase of the journey we were issued with the SA80 assault rifle. The troop had been given the task of testing the weapon in order to see how it performed in desert conditions.

The SA80 was extremely different from the SLR. The length was shorter and the ammunition was 5.56mm rather than 7.62mm. On first impressions it felt rather comfortable, it looked impressive and had the added advantage of an optical sight. The ammunition was Nato compatible and because of its smaller calibre more of it could be carried.

The drills on the weapon commenced and I looked forward to the chance of firing it.

Landing in Cyprus via the ship's Sea Kings, we set up camp in a tented city a few miles from Limassol. The weather was rather chilly and before I knew it I was out in the field patrolling the local hills. The exercise wasn't particularly hard but I developed my map and patrolling skills. The landscape was plain, barren and sun-baked in appearance.

True to form, not long after I began to stretch my legs the heavens opened and it began to rain heavily. This lasted for a number of days, soaking everything and everyone.

It was at this stage that I began to notice a number of problems with the SA80. Due to the damp and colder conditions, I found that every time I used the optical sight the glass lens steamed over from the heat of my eye. This made it difficult to identify targets in firefights and OPs. The working parts which helped to eject the brass cylinders quickly jammed because ventilation slits allowed in extra dust and grit. This became even worse when I was caught in the downdraught of a Sea King.

The exercises enabled us to practise and get an idea of what was going to be required when we eventually landed in Oman. Most of us chose not to carry sleeping bags and extra clothing because we wanted to be able to carry extra water. The nights were uncomfortable as we were wet and our jungle lightweight clothing didn't retain any heat.

Back at Tent City, we reported on how the SA80 had

initially performed over this brief exercise. At this stage I assumed that our recommendations would then be looked at. This was never the case and the weapon remained very much the same when it eventually replaced the SLR in Commando units.

The runs ashore in Limassol were quieter because it was out of the tourist season, but this didn't stop me from doing my own thing, like renting a motorbike and bumming around on the beach.

I was now completely settled in the troop and had made a number of good friends whilst living on the mess deck. Jim, from Bristol, had the bunk above me. He loved his beer when given the chance and was very funny with it. He had a similar personality to mine and I found him very genuine and easy to get on with. Scouse and Dinger also appeared to get on with Jim, which resulted in us always going ashore together.

On one particular night things didn't go quite accordingly to plan. No sooner had we gone ashore in Limassol than Dinger discovered he had lost his wallet. He immediately got a 'shitty on' because he was worried about losing his ID card and quickly returned to camp.

We then spent the remainder of the night visiting local haunts until I vaguely remembered coming round in what appeared to be a back street café. Glancing at my watch, I realised it was well past four in the morning. As I lifted my head from the table and got to my feet, I suddenly felt dizzy. While I battled to remain conscious, I discovered from the muffled surroundings that I had lost the hearing in my right ear. My mind was now racing to establish what was going on. Placing my finger against my ear, I felt liquid running down the side of my face. This unnatural sensation made me nervous about where I was and what was wrong with me.

I thought, Who had hit me? Was I badly injured? I needed to get help!

Staggering around, I didn't initially recognise anybody among the people gazing at me.

I was now sobering up fairly quickly and I heard the muffled sounds of Jim and Scouse's laughter. At least they hadn't left me. They were propped up at the far end of the bar, obviously enjoying themselves. But why weren't they helping me?

Feeling slightly better in the knowledge of their presence I turned to the table in order to collect my belongings and quickly realised why they were laughing. Because of the position that I had fallen asleep in, Jim had decided to pour tomato sauce into my ear as I slept. There was in fact nothing wrong with me other than being slightly the worse for wear and having an earful of tomato sauce!

Back on board *Intrepid*, I spent the next two weeks of the tour picking lumps of dried tomato sauce from my ear.

The days were passing slowly when we eventually arrived at Port Suez, Egypt at the north end of the Suez Canal.

I had booked in advance to go on an organised trip to Cairo, so, disembarking with Jim and Scouse, I clambered aboard a tatty-looking mini-bus and settled for the overnight journey to the capital. Egypt seemed extremely busy in the built-up towns we passed, but there were also miles and miles of desert holding a few local tribes with a number of camels.

Arriving in Cairo, we attempted to book into our hotel. This turned out to be a shambles, as they didn't seem to be able to accommodate us all. It was now in the early hours and a few harsh words were said before I managed to get my head down.

In the morning, used to the lack of sleep, we all set off for the Pyramids on our guided tour. My expectations were high, I had seen and read so much about them over the years. As we drove to this great wonder of the world, I reflected on my hard times at CTC. This was what I had joined for, travel.

Our mini-bus soon became surrounded on the hectic city roads. The streets were dry and dirty, baked by the scorching sun for the best part of the day. Building line after building line cast shadows across the streets as local people carried out their daily chores. People and traffic moved in all directions. There didn't appear to be any rules of the road. Taxis and carts grappled continually for the best routes through the sea of traffic.

Travelling across the city, I noticed the vast amount of ditches and canals that bordered the back roads. They appeared to be filthy, full of discarded rubbish and devoid of any kind of life. Then the cranky mini-bus turned up what appeared to be another dishevelled road. This wasn't the case because from between the drab buildings the Pyramids began to appear before me.

Because of my high expectations I found them rather disappointing and a bit of an anti-climax. I felt conned by all the hype and my own imagination. To my young eye they appeared like fixed piles of rubble, dumped in the desert. What made it worse was the pestering locals. There were bands of scavengers – not animals but human beings. They congregated around any unsuspecting tourist in desperate attempts to sell their wares. They even tried to charge me for taking a picture of their camels. My patience with them soon ran low.

The Sphinx, located close by, also had a tired weathered expression on its noseless face.

Finally, after tempers began to fray, we quickly gathered for a souvenir photograph and clambered back on our bus.

The remainder of the day was spent touring and visiting museums. I detested the place as I was herded from one venue to the next.

By the end of the trip, when our mini-bus entered Port Said at the south end of the Suez Canal, I was tired and fed up with the heckling. *Intrepid* had sailed through the canal with the remainder of the crew and we met her here. I was glad to see her again and even happier to be leaving Egypt. All my memories of the place were bad, but this was probably to do with my outlook on life at the time.

Once we were back in the sanctuary of *Intrepid*, the ship continued on her journey, this time heading for Djibouti on the east coast of Africa. During this part of the journey the troop took the opportunity to do some live firing with the SA80 off the stern of the ship. Rubbish bags thrown overboard gave us something to aim at initially. When these ran out we resorted to blowing up condoms and half filling them with water. These made great flotation markers but the blue ones were harder to spot!

Whilst we were live firing with the SA80 in these calm and sunny conditions, it performed rather well. But this didn't ease my doubts on how it would perform in desert and field conditions.

The weather was now becoming rather hot. In the evenings I would go up on deck to relax and watch the world go sailing by. It was times like these as the sun was setting behind the horizon that I began to think about life and where it would be taking me. At this point money wasn't important. I had enough of it to keep me happy.

In a way I was glad to be away from our materialistic society.

My mind wandered and wondered as I daydreamed, staring out at the distant horizon. I did on occasions miss having a female companion. I didn't have time for long relationships back in England. I sometimes thought it would have been nice to have a letter from a girl now and then. But, never mind, it wasn't to be.

During one of these periods of relaxation I had the pleasure of watching dolphins jumping across the front of the ship, riding the pressure wave. They seemed so happy and free leaping across the bow of the ship oblivious to the danger.

The short distance to reach Djibouti was covered quickly. The port was like many Third World docks: deserted, dirty and somewhat dangerous. Nobody was allowed to travel through the docks alone or on foot.

Djibouti was the main supply route for food into the country. Food and supplies for Ethiopia were also delivered via this port, and people carried out desperate acts to get these valuable resources, so the entrances and main roads were guarded by government troops equipped with the infamous AK47 assault rifle.

Looking at the squalor and poverty on land, I wasn't in a rush to get ashore and have a pint.

We spent an afternoon at hands to bathe (swimming) on the ramp at the end of the ship. The only unnerving point was when the shark/safety boat came out. Two dolphins attracted to all the laughing and splashing were the closest I came to seeing sharks on this day. A couple of Marines, Nobby included, decided to jump from the side of *Intrepid*, which didn't impress the duty officer.

The next day we were allowed to use a camp occupied by a French Foreign Legion unit. Their base was close to the shore but swimming was limited owing to the amount of coral and sharks in the sea.

During the day the temperature became unbearable at times, but this didn't stop us from having a barbecue on a beach. We travelled to this beach by four-ton truck and the chefs prepared the scran (food). The scran and beer was great; however, the sun was incredibly hot, burning my unprotected skin in a few minutes if allowed.

At the end of the day we returned to ship through the local settlements. As we passed by in our vehicles, the children would just stand still and stare blankly at us. None of them appeared to possess any clean items of clothing. The shoes on their feet were weathered and worn. Their dark African faces revealed little or no emotion and a smile was hard to find. I couldn't help noticing how sad they looked.

Every time we travelled through the local settlements I began to realise how much our Western lifestyle differed from theirs. Toilets didn't seem to exist. They would just squat at the side of the street and go for a shit. This resulted in contamination of water supplies and increased the spread of disease. To me the lack of hygiene was obvious, but the locals didn't seem aware of it. I felt pity for the children and the circumstances they had been born into through no fault of their own.

I couldn't seem to solve this problem but I certainly had time to think about it as *Intrepid* headed out to sea again.

As the hot sunny days passed I started to become ill, very ill. I was constantly sick, day and night, unable to keep anything down. The mere suggestion of food or liquid made me vomit. My strength began to fail as I became weaker and weaker from dehydration. It eventually got to the stage where I couldn't get out of bed and felt as if I was going to die.

The ship's medical officer gave me some drugs to settle my stomach but this seemed to have little effect initially. I was given bed rest as the days passed slowly.

Lying in my bunk, I watched the lads preparing for another landing, this time by Sea Kings to the island of Masira. I was too ill to do anything and deeply depressed at missing the chance to get ashore. I felt rather isolated being left on ship when the troop disembarked, and I quickly discovered that I was alone apart from two other lads who were in a worse condition than me.

After 24 hours I couldn't take any more. The boredom of the deserted ship and the thought of what the lads were doing took over. I had to get ashore! I wasn't completely fit but my enthusiasm to rejoin the troop made up for this. The weather up on deck was also fantastic and this assisted in my recovery from what turned out to be a severe dose of gastro-enteritis.

Eventually, after a lot of persuasion, the ship's sergeant major agreed that I could join my section on the next re-supply flight.

Grabbing my kit together, I clambered aboard the next available flight. The Sea Kings were making regular water-supply flights so, after loading a number of jerry cans, I sat back to enjoy the flight.

As it left the ship's flight deck, the Sea King strained to get airborne. The noise inside the military helicopter was deafening but highly motivating.

The pilot took us across the open ocean and, realising that he had time to spare, decided to try and impress his co-pilot.

This turned out to be my first real experience of aggressive flying. Up, down around and around the machine went. I was surprised how manoeuvrable the aircraft was, especially considering the amount of extra weight it was carrying. One moment I felt weightless looking into the air and the next moment I was staring at the blue sea below.

After a while the man who seemed to be temporarily holding my life in his hands brought the aircraft to a hover. My attention was then drawn to the sea below, where I saw the largest hammerhead shark I had ever set eyes on. It must have been close to 15 feet in length as it swam just below the surface of the crystal-clear water. The thought of engine failure and ditching in the sea didn't seem to be very attractive now!

Half an hour later the winchman gave me the signal that we were approaching the drop-off point. Preparing myself for the landing, I grabbed my kit and jumped off. My eyes were protected by a pair of goggles from the blinding sand whipped up by the helicopter. Particles of grit did manage to get into my goggles, but without them it would have been impossible to see. I felt as if I had been sand-blasted when the aircraft departed.

I quickly found my colleagues from the troop and established where my own section were. Finding them under makeshift hessian shelters, I saw they already appeared to be shattered and suffering from the effects of the sun.

After pairing off with Scouse, I soon established that they had been spending most of the time acclimatising to the heat. Before long I satisfied myself that I hadn't jumped ship too soon. Then the sun was on its way down for the night, the magnificent sunset revealing a mixture of oranges and reds that I had seen only on television.

No sooner had the sun slid behind the horizon than the

temperature began to drop. Doing my turns on the sentry position, I found the still air became very cold in the early hours. But it was uncomfortable rather than unbearable.

I instantly settled into my routine and subsequently had an easy first night whilst another section went out on a recce patrol. The starlit night made visibility very good. I could clearly make out shapes and silhouettes from quite a distance away. I discovered that our night vision devices were excellent, especially when viewing across open ground. This made it very simple to see a man walking and thus he would be an easy target.

Lying on the dry desert sand with a hessian sheet as my only outside protection, I began to gaze at the stars. In total silence I stared blankly at the incredible array of lights above. I tried to identify various cluster formations of stars like the Bear, Plough and Orion's belt. Moments like this made me realise who and what I was in this huge place thousands of miles from loved ones.

My illness was now behind me, but the feeling of being on dry land made me much happier for the time being.

All our operations for the remainder of the exercise were carried out at night, owing to the incredible heat during the day. From an operational and tactical point of view it was far better to lie up for the day than stand out like a sore thumb on this very barren landscape. Most of the day was spent lying out of the sun under a hessian blanket one foot off the ground. This saved valuable energy and reduced water consumption.

Water was now the most important asset I possessed. On average it was easy to consume eight pints of water a day. This created a massive demand on our own re-supply sources, which in turn affected the way that we could operate. It was very easy to drink lots of water but this created more sweat, turning the whole process of drinking water into a vicious circle. I had to use great self-discipline.

The temptation to empty my bottle was great, but I soon became accustomed to taking small sips, which turned out to be the best method of quenching my thirst.

Another routine I quickly picked up was the process of drinking water in the morning. Its icy temperature first thing bore no comparison to later on in the day when it tasted warm and insipid. Come the end of the exercise I had perfected my own basic field craft skills that personally suited me.

One problem I did have, though, was that sand had encrusted my body in every imaginable place. This, combined with strenuous activities, had caused sores where skin and kit had chafed. I was going to have to be aware of this problem and cover vulnerable parts like my hips.

Reloading back onto *Intrepid* took time but we only had a couple of days to spare before the main landings in the Republic of Oman.

During the time back on board we rehearsed the landing procedure and had an operational briefing from our troop boss. Our part involved cross-decking to HMS *Illustrious*, which was now sailing with us. *Illustrious* was an operational aircraft carrier which carried Sea Harriers and anti-submarine Sea King helicopters.

These Sea Kings, which were different in design from the normal troop-carrying Sea King, were required to ferry us ashore on the morning of the assault. They could only hold half the cargo because of the extra sonar equipment they carried.

After the short, uneventful flight to *Illustrious*, we were shown where we would have to wait below deck. The design of this rather large ship was impressive. Two hydraulic lifts incorporated into the flight deck were the main ways in which aircraft and large bodies of Marines moved below deck.

The basic plan for the landing was to ferry as many men ashore as quickly and easily as possible.

We familiarised ourselves briefly with the ship, then we visited the bridge and discovered how this complex vessel was controlled.

During this short visit I was impressed by how efficiently the operations were conducted. It was a web of organisation, enabling planes and men to work in unison to achieve the same goal. I watched in astonishment as Sea Harriers landed and took off, the pilots manoeuvring the aircraft with immense skill and co-ordination as the ship rolled in the open sea.

After flying back to *Intrepid* I finished preparing my kit and took time to relax before the final briefing. My buddy for the exercise was going to be Dave. This gave me great comfort because he was a lot older than me. From my experiences in Cyprus and previous exercises he appeared to be highly proficient in the field. He carried the LMG (light machine gun) for the section, which made me his No 2.

Dave had moved to our section during a slight reorganisation of the troop. He had joined the Corp relatively late in life. A mechanic by trade, he was rather quiet but self-confident. During our conversations on ship he told me that he had joined up because he needed a change in his lifestyle.

Later that evening we reached the shores off the Oman coast, and shortly after dark we moved to the flight deck, waiting to be transported back to HMS *Illustrious*. Exercise 'Siaf Sareea' had begun.

It was a lovely warm still evening when I clambered aboard the Sea King. During this short trip I noticed how shiny and frozen the surface of the sea appeared to be, as it reflected the starlit night.

Landing between a variety of coloured lights on HMS *Illustrious*, we climbed from the aircraft and were led down to the hangar below. I attempted to grab a few hours' sleep but, prior to first light and with no success, we mustered into our flight sticks [boarding groups].

The sight that greeted me as we were raised on the hydraulic flight deck was impressive. Sea Kings appeared to be nose to tail along the entire length of the deck. The noise was deafening as their rotor blades slashed into the air. I climbed aboard my allocated aircraft with Dave directly in front of me and dumped my small Bergen at the rear of the aircraft.

Taking off in sequence, we flew directly towards the beach. By now the sun was beginning to rise, revealing the start of another hot day. The landing was going to be un-opposed because the two other companies had been ferried ashore to secure the beach. As the wheels of the aircraft touched the ground the side door opened, exposing a sea of airborne sand. The goggles over my eyes gave me some protection as I charged through the shield of grit and dived to the nearest piece of cover whilst holding a Bergen in one hand and an SA80 in the other.

Quickly finding Dave, I could hear muffled gunfire in the distance. Fortunately we didn't have any directed at us so there was no need to flap.

As we orientated ourselves to the ground I noticed four Hercules transport planes flying over us about 500 feet up. These carried members of the Parachute Regiment who had flown straight from Cyprus. This all added to the realism as I prepared for my first contact with the local militia.

The morning quickly passed and I found myself walking during the hottest part of the day. The amount of equipment I carried was minimal but the excessive heat was oppressing, the yomp to our RV point was a considerable distance. I began to hit that stage of incipient heat exhaustion as my mind began to wander with each subsequent step.

The second in command of the company, Lieutenant Garrard, soon began to realise that he was going to lose a number of men if the pace continued. So when we found suitable cover we moved into a lie-up position for the remainder of the afternoon.

During the earlier part of the morning I had glanced at the passing countryside, which evidently had seen little sign of water for many weeks. The land was mountainous with large areas of plains. The only vegetation was a gorse-type tussock bush sparsely covering the lower ground. The ground was extremely hard under foot because of its sun-baked condition. It was also covered in an abundance of rocks as far as the eye could see. This increased the likelihood of turning an ankle, and the Parachute Regiment members who jumped in from the passing C-130 Hercules sustained a number of injuries from the rocky terrain.

Map-reading, however, was rather easier than in some of the places I had covered during previous exercises. This was of course dependent on the maps we used and when they were printed.

*   *   *

The exercise proved rather intensive, with most of the efforts being carried out at night. After the initial landing ashore, movement was dramatically reduced. Our section spent several nights on recce patrols identifying Omani positions. This was hard, because of the bright nights and the optical equipment the Omani were believed to possess.

One night, from our dusty confines, we watched a large congregation of troops from a mountain ridge using image-intensifying equipment. I couldn't help giggling to myself as they stood around chatting, totally unaware of our presence. The satisfaction of getting the job right was great. Of course, this information would be passed back through the chains of command at the patrol de-brief.

The exercise was passing quickly and I had little time to get my camera out for sentimental poses.

At the end of the sixth day I prepared for a night in a troop harbour position. On this occasion we had taken up a position on the edge of a dried-up wadi. Eating my main evening meal, I noticed the build-up of clouds and the distant sound of thunder over the nearby mountains. Nobody, myself included, thought it might rain in this hot and dry country, so I settled down for a few hours' sleep.

Shortly after nodding off, I was awoken by the feeling of cold rain against my face. Initially I lay there trying not to think about the droplets but they rapidly began to develop into a downpour. Within minutes I was soaking and the dry wadi was now trickling with water. Picking up my weapon and shuffling to higher ground, I watched as the water quickly turned into a knee-deep river. The noise from the flowing water began to increase as it raced by my thighs. This was interspersed with concerned shouts from people as they collected their kit and accounted for everybody who should have been with them. It was rather darker than previous nights because of the cloud cover. I checked the nearest lads to me – Scouse, Dave and Dinger – to ascertain they were awake and all right.

The troop boss seemed to realise the serious position we were in and instructed us to move up onto some high ground. The water was now flowing very fast; it was above my waist and rising. Gripping each other's kit, we moved across the low ground towards the nearby ridge. It was now every man for himself as we stumbled in the fast-flowing muddy water to our sanctuary. The sight of two submerged Land Rovers would have been unbelievable an hour earlier. Thankfully, there were no fatalities, but lots of equipment was swept away, never to be seen again. The speed with which the water had filled the wadi was amazing and quite frightening. Eventually the rain stopped and we had time to take stock of what had happened.

Next morning small amounts of water remained as evidence of our potentially dangerous night.

Before long we moved into the final assault, which passed without incident. I then took time to relax and catch my breath whilst we awaited transport back to ship, courtesy of the Oman troops.

After a long and bone-shaking journey we arrived at the beachhead. The sea looked very tempting indeed, especially when I was told the flight back to *Intrepid* was going to be delayed. The idea of a quick dip was put forward but to our horror we weren't allowed in. This was owing to the local turtles having right of way!

Sitting on the beach, I noticed that one of our Sea Kings had lost a landing wheel and was attempting to land back on *Intrepid*. The ship was making various turns into the oncoming wind to accommodate the aircraft, but the risk of the Sea King crashing was great. It made several attempts to land on a makeshift ramp which the flight deck crew had quickly assembled to support the aircraft. Fortunately, after a considerable amount of effort and time, the helicopter landed safely on the flight deck.

This incident, coupled with my own experiences of flying in Sea Kings, highlighted how proficient our brigade pilots were.

Back on board I immediately began to count the days down as we set sail full steam for England. As Christmas approached the journey back was slow and painful at times. It encompassed most of the countries I had visited on the way out, and our first run ashore was in Gibraltar.

This turned into a release of tension after the weeks we had been stuck on ship. During the night, like everyone else, I had far too much to drink. Unsurprisingly this was a recipe for trouble and it soon came, outside a bar, in the form of locals. In the confusion that followed I was certainly not proud of my behaviour. From my recollection of events, I witnessed a friend being attacked, so I jumped to his defence, as any Marine would have done. The next thing chaos erupted in the street. I found myself rolling around fighting with somebody. I wasn't even aware if this man was responsible for striking my oppo. All I knew was that if I stayed on the floor the law of averages stated that I would come off worse.

A few punches to my face later, I stumbled to my feet when I suddenly found myself being pushed forward and handcuffed. I began to sober up quickly as I was marched away and out of the fighting. Seconds after this I saw the local police station and quickly arrived at the cell compound.

I wasn't alone as a few other lads from the troop were in the cell with me.

What was I doing? I soon realised that I had behaved like a right arsehole.

There was a lot of trouble taking place that night and the local bobbies were struggling to cope. The cell compound was full of drunken idiots, of whom I was one. Eventually the shore patrol turned up with the RSM and a small negotiation seemed to take place. The next thing, I was being released and herded into a Transit van. From here the shore patrol ferried us back to ship, where we were put in a transit room to await our punishment in the morning.

Come the new dawn our behaviour was identified by the RSM and that was the end of my shore leave for the three days the ship remained in port. I remained on board working and sporting a nice black eye, whilst the rest of the troop who had behaved themselves or not got caught spent another two days ashore.

Eventually, after what seemed like a lifetime, Plymouth and England arrived. It had been my first long period away from home so I didn't need any encouragement to race back for Christmas.

6

HARDSHIP, HORNETS AND MONKEYS

As I settled down and grew accustomed to the frequent trips abroad, my commitment towards the Corps was total and I was enjoying life tremendously.

Back at Taunton, having successfully completed the annual weapons test at Altcar ranges near Southport, I found myself donning a pair of football boots. Football was my childhood passion, and there was a possibility of getting into one of the two unit football teams.

The trials were about getting your face noticed amongst the more senior lads in the unit. Two PTI colour sergeants from the unit organised the various training sessions, and at the finish I was selected for the under 19s team. I was delighted. It meant I had a chance to relax for two weeks and concentrate on playing football and winning the 'Tunny Cup'.

The tournament was held at Royal Marines, Deal, in Kent the home of the Corps Band. We (the U19s team) took a back seat in order to train, whilst the senior team endeavoured to reach the next round in the competition. Dedicated to the end, the team took in the sights and sounds of Deal. The relaxed attitude enabled me to meet new companions from the unit and old friends from CTCRM.

The senior team were soon eliminated from the competition, and quickly returned to Taunton.

Fortunately, we had progressed to the final of the Navy Cup. Moving to 'Pompey' (Portsmouth) we stayed in the Corps' most historic barracks, Royal Marines, Eastney.

I took the opportunity to walk around the famous museum. It was crammed with exhibits about historic events from the successful capture and defence of Gibraltar in 1704 to Corporal Hunter's VC at Lake Commanchio in 1945. I felt proud of being part of this immense family history. Even now, words cannot describe what it is like to have been a serving Royal Marine Commando.

The day of the final took us to a small local football stadium, which engulfed the few supporters who had bothered to turn up.

The pre-match briefing from the colour sergeant team manager was straightforward and to the point, but the first half was a very scrappy affair and resulted in a bollocking at half time for our lack of spirit and commitment.

Consequently the second half was entirely different and we quickly scored to take us ahead. From then on, our fitness dominated against the not-so-fit Navy side and we scored a number of times again before the final whistle, eventually winning 8–2.

We had won the 1986 Navy Cup! Needless to say, the celebrations were somewhat excessive but thoroughly deserved.

The two weeks of football had given me the taste of what life for a professional player must have been like, minus the pay. My performances had earned me selection for the Navy side on a tour to Dallas, America.

However, there was one catch. B Company were due to go away jungle training in Brunei and I had to make a decision about which trip I wanted to embark on: playing football in Dallas, USA, or jungle warfare training in the Far East.

It was easy – jungle warfare training. I hadn't joined to play football. I wanted the challenge of working in a team whilst under pressure in an extremely hostile environment.

I quickly found myself queuing in the company store, waiting to collect my jungle kit. The store was a damp and dusty place which had a counter just inside the wooden doorframe. Behind the counter was an immense array of equipment, ranging from magazines to American-style jungle boots.

Colour Sergeant Evans and two senior Marines ran the store. Other than deploying into the field, life for these two Marines was fairly cushy because of all the extra benefits that came with the job.

Reaching the counter, I was thrown a metal-framed Bergen and instructed to check off the items it contained. I noticed it even included luxury features like an Australian lightweight shelter, a metal mug and a new pair of size 8 American jungle boots, which were far superior to the British alternative. The boot was made from a mixture of canvas and leather with a water outlet hole in each instep. Inside the sole was a metal plate designed to protect the wearer from boobytraps.

Having amassed all my equipment, I was told that the troop was going to embark on a short exercise on Dartmoor. The spring sunshine at Taunton persuaded me, against my better judgement to take very little in the way of warm clothing.

Having hastily assembled my kit, I was soon climbing aboard a Sea King. During the flight I took in the passing scenery, as the cold breeze coming from the open cargo door was slightly masked by the hot air from the engines of the helicopter.

The distance from camp to Dartmoor was covered

quickly and I was soon jumping into wet, knee-deep tussock grass. Diving behind the nearest mound of cover, I heard the noise from the helicopters slowly fade as they swiftly hurried towards the far horizon.

I soon began to regain my senses and switch on to the new surroundings. Lying close to a cold rocky outcrop, I quickly realised that I was once again in a very lonely and isolated location.

Waiting for some kind of notification to move, I began to ponder on what lay ahead. I stared at the passing clouds, watching them cluster together and darken in colour. They seemed to gel into one another, giving me the impression it definitely wanted to rain.

The hostile cloud movements confirmed that the weather was extremely unpredictable in this part of the country. But, pushing the thought of wet weather to the back of my mind, I motivated myself to the task I was supposed to be concentrating on.

We spent the day moving from location to location until we reached a final rendezvous position. On the side of a barren and exposed feature we were given time to prepare a quick meal before last light. A night recce patrol was then sent out.

I remained in the troop harbour position to await their return. The weather temperature had dropped dramatically and frost began to coat every exposed surface. My feet were freezing in my new boots, aggravated by the metal plate in the sole. The exercise was only memorable because of the cold and the discovery that US jungle boots let in vast amounts of Dartmoor water. Not the ideal preparation for jungle warfare training.

*   *   *

Before flying to Brunei we had the opportunity to spend seven days in Hong Kong acclimatisation training. This turned out to be a great time. In the day we carried out various sporting events and the odd yomp around the mainland coast. But by night we were given a free rein to have a run ashore, spending the early part of the evening shopping and walking around Temple Street night market.

One particular night I couldn't even recall getting back to our camp, Osbourne Barracks. My last vision, was a seedy bar where I had been drinking vodka and watching dancing girls with Scouse and Mick. These nights turned out to be rather expensive because most of the items I had purchased were normally lost or left behind in bars.

The troop had been together for quite a while and morale was high. Whilst in Hong Kong we took part in various inter-service competitions. The company side beat the resident Coldstream Guards battalion at rugby, although most confrontations took place on the sidelines between rival fans. We also had a sports day with the Gurkhas, which proved to be very enjoyable.

We arrived in Brunei at the beginning of March to a temperature of 30°C, blue skies and a hammering sun.

A hot and cramped coach ride brought us to Sitang Camp, which was situated close to the sea and the river Tutong. The camp was very basic. It consisted of open-sided sleeping quarters that were stuffy when occupied by numerous sweaty Marines, a shower block and canteen.

From the beginning we adopted an early start at Sitang, a long lunch and a late finish. The morning always began with a run, which was fantastic. It got me going and concluded on the white sandy beach a hundred yards from

147

camp. Swimming in the sea on a beautiful beach at 06.00 hours surpassed everything I had done in the Corps.

The week that followed was spent in acclimatisation training. This included instruction on jungle equipment, HF (high frequency) radio, codes, helicopter familiarisation, basic jungle navigation and first aid revision such as putting clean venflons [intravenous needles] into each other's arms. The week also included fundamental section routines which sharpened our skills in the hostile environment. (Section routines were common tasks carried out in the field, like eating, digging defensive positions and cleaning weapons.)

At the end of the first week we moved into the 'Jungle School', which was located in primary jungle a few miles from Sitang. Once we were there, the training became intense; we were taught everything from how to live off the land to constructing basic and complex survival shelters. The use of booby traps, setting snares and ambushes were only a few of the tasks we had to carry out. I was even given the opportunity to blow up a few trees with plastic explosives.

The local Iban tribesmen educated us in survival. They were head-hunters and absolutely at home in the forest. They passed on their tracking expertise, identifying what we should look for, from broken foliage to muddy footprints under water at the edge of a water source and down to the smallest sign indicating a booby trap. I was even given the doubtful pleasure of eating barbecued monkey and snake, which tasted predominately of charcoal.

My first night under the canopy was an experience in itself. Beasties and bugs seemed to be everywhere. Just before last light the jungle seemed to erupt with the noise of animals and insects. The sound was deafening at times and hard to imagine unless heard for real. Even the toughest found it difficult to sleep soundly on the floor of the jungle on their first night.

One night I was awoken from my sleep in the pitch-black to blood-curdling screaming. The sound of a man screaming in pain is very distinctive. At first I had no idea what had happened but soon learned that one of the lads from another section had fallen asleep and a baby hornet had somehow got stuck in his ear. He was mad with pain because every time he moved, the hornet stung him again. At the end of a long night he had to be flown out by helicopter for hospital treatment.

Live firing was also an experience. The targets were difficult to identify, but I had a good natural eye for being able to see through the jungle and spot the targets. We practised on a variety of weapons: AR15s, M203s, which were AR15s with a grenade launcher attached to the bottom of the stock, LMGs and our standard SLRs.

With our new skills, the operations over the following weeks got longer, taking us deeper into the jungle. Some of the areas we spent time in were scenic and a long way from civilisation. I loved it.

We crammed the little time off full of activities. One trip followed an invitation to spend the day at a leisure complex owned by a British oil company. A game of football was arranged with the expats, and I even managed to score. It turned out to be a very welcome break and the hospitality of our hosts was exceptional. During another break I had the chance to learn wind surfing and snorkelling on a freshwater lake.

A few of the lads decided to do different things, and one particular group, which included Carl, went water skiing on a river. He had taken up a seat at the front end of the boat, waiting for his turn to get into the water. A few lads were in the boat with him, whilst the remainder of the party waited on the riverbank with the four-ton truck. The boat was making runs up and down the river and everybody had grown accustomed to the routine of fallers. During one fall the boat turned sharply in the water to collect the skier. The manoeuvre caught Carl unawares; he fell backwards out of the boat into the water. In the split seconds that followed Carl disappeared into the brown water and the boat crossed over the top. Exploding to the surface he let out an almighty scream, 'I've lost my legs, I've lost my legs!'

Instinctively and without fear for themselves, a few lads dived into the water to keep him afloat. As he was encircled by a dark bloody patch, it was quite obvious that he was badly injured. When Carl was pulled from the water, his injuries proved to be far worse than anyone could have imagined. The propeller had sliced clean through one leg, leaving just a piece of tissue connecting it to his thigh. His other leg was just as bad; only the majority of muscle from one side held it together. Carl was close to death and desperately needed hospital treatment.

The lads' training kicked in and towels and any other suitable items were used to stem the bleeding. Frantically dragging him from the boat and onto the bank, they quickly threw him into the back of the four-ton truck. Carl began drifting in and out of consciousness. All they could do was keep him awake and prevent any further blood loss. The journey to the nearest hospital was along some very bad roads but there was no way anything was going to slow them down. Getting to the hospital some 30 minutes after the accident, the lads began donating their own matched blood groups, making transfusions available to Carl. The ensuing hours in theatre were touch and go, but Carl survived, owing to the effective first aid given by his colleagues.

I later took time to visit Carl in a local hospital and saw how devastated he was when he realised that he had lost one of his legs. However, despite being very seriously ill, Carl amazed us all by his rapid recovery and became an inspiration to us by his determination and courage to face his sudden disability. He was flown back to England with his family and I never saw him again.

Eventually we were ready to embark on our final exercise, which would take us away from civilisation for 16 days. The idea of the operation was to clear ridgelines, locate the enemy, conduct close target recces and then attack and destroy the camps. My buddy for the next two weeks was Brendan, a new member to the section who had a strong south-west accent. He was fairly experienced in the jungle, having completed a tour of Belize a year earlier.

The exercise was a complete experience: hard times, funny times and interesting times. It took us across a wide variety of terrains and into the Sukang Belait swamp region of mangrove forests. Normally under three to four feet of water, the swamps were drier than normal, exposing roots and creepers which created a major obstacle when we were moving. Map-reading was important, although the maps were not that accurate, because the contour lines played a very important part in deciding a route. The dense jungle made it difficult to recognise mountains on the ground: they only became apparent when breathing and heart rates increased. And we always avoided tracks because of the threat of ambushes.

The exercise was extremely well run and incorporated travelling by boat to tactical river crossings. I didn't particularly relish these. The thought of the crocodiles lurking at the bottom made me very apprehensive. Even having a spotter on the bank acting like Crocodile Dundee didn't help to reassure me. Half-sunken, swollen trees were also a major danger to the boats, and us.

We carried all our equipment with us but got the occasional food re-supply. Waiting for the helicopter, we would cut a winch hole in the tree canopy in order for food to be lowered.

By the second week our dirty, unshaven appearance gave us a rather bedraggled look but we had started to function perfectly. Western smells like soap and deodorant were never used as they could linger in the jungle air, giving away a position. Although tired, I was enjoying myself in the testing conditions. I was certainly a Marine for the tropics and not the cold.

One early morning we set up a harbour position in the vicinity of an enemy longhouse, which had been occupied by our mock freedom-fighters. It was close to the top of Bukit Teraja, which at 1,367 feet is the highest peak in Brunei. The previous day had been spent conducting close-target recces on the area to establish their size, weapons and routines. We attacked the target at dawn. This started well but in the confusion a pyrotechnic set the longhouse on fire. Its timber construction and dry roof burst into flames and the chaos that followed was somewhat frightening for some of the lads. Bergens cached prior to the attack were destroyed or damaged by a fire that had almost encircled us and was getting closer and closer. We only just managed to traverse a fallen tree before the fire destroyed the riverbank we vacated only seconds before.

During the second week I awoke to my eighteenth birthday, but I somehow felt older in my present surroundings. I had planned from the outset of the exercise to give the lads in the section something to smile about. Diving to the depths of my Bergen, I produced four cans of Tiger beer. Like the water in our bottles, it was coldest first thing in the morning. It tasted great, especially for breakfast!

Completely shattered and able to smell my own body odour, I was happy to hear end ex. My clothing had started to rot from the perpetual dampness. I was covered in bites from an assortment of insects. The mosquito repellent and locally purchased Tiger Balm had little effect in easing the uncomfortable condition because of constant perspiration. The temperature change when I walked from underneath the jungle canopy into the direct sunlight outside was blistering. It took my eyes a few moments to adjust to the brightness of the sun as if I had just come out of a darkened room.

Moving back to Sitang Camp I had a welcome wash and shave but, more importantly, Danny, Scouse and I had other plans. Before leaving on the final exercise we had been informed that we had a week's R and R after the exercise, and the company sergeant major had managed to arrange (courtesy of Royal Brunei Airways) a cheap package tour to Thailand.

Arriving in Bangkok, we never looked back. I made up for my lack of eighteenth birthday celebrations. The seven of us who took up the adventure had a wild partying time. Bangkok was hustle and bustle, with people everywhere. Then, after a couple of days in Bangkok itself, we left our fine hotel for a rickety old bus and embarked on a journey to Patyua, on the coast. Once there, I adopted a typical beach bum mode, lying about the beach all day, jet skiing and swimming. Having spent the last 16 days away from civilisation, I had earned the rest and recuperation period. At night it was party, party, party.

Coming back to England was a big anti-climax. I found it hard to settle back into the camp routine and missed the tropics. I had to do something different and quickly, especially as the football had dried up because of my decision to turn the Navy down and go to Brunei.

Walking back from the galley one evening, I noticed a draft request for Marines to volunteer for the Brigade Dog Section in Plymouth. Without giving it much thought I put in for the draft the following morning. It came through very quickly and within a few days I was saying goodbye to the lads at Norton Manor camp. I never saw them again.

On the way to the RAVC (Royal Army Veterinary Corps) training centre for the two-week course I met Wally. He, too, had been in B Company and although I didn't know him well we hit it off straight away. We were the only two Marines on the mixed service course run by the Army. The course was basic, to say the least, and uneventful – other than being bitten by vicious dogs.

Every night Wally and I went ashore in Melton Mowbray. Two airborne forces lads were also on the course and we became good drinking pals for the duration. The two weeks were typically Army – lots of shouting and by the book. I hated it, apart from the run ashore.

Having successfully completed the training, I moved back to my new draft, the Royal Marines Dog Section at Stonehouse Barracks, Plymouth. The section at any one time ranged from seven to ten Marines in strength and was organised by two corporals and a sergeant. As always, we rarely had two corporals and Sergeant Ozzy didn't have much to do with us. Ozzy was a very senior sergeant who had seen service in Aden. He was daft as a brush, very kind-hearted and looking forward to his retirement. The corporal we had most of the time was completely different and I found it hard to like the man. He was self-opinionated, full of his self-importance and even fuller of nonsense stories. The tales were always longer and better than anyone else's. He was the original black cat. Wally and I continually took the piss out of him.

The primary role of the dog section was to act as battle line casualty replacements for the brigade in time of conflict, but our peacetime role was camp security.

I was now an REMF (Rear Echelon Mother Fucker) watching the units go out on deployments while I stayed back in Plymouth. This meant I had a terrific social life with some of the lads from my unit. Wally and I were the only single lads on the section, so we worked our shifts together to accommodate our social life. Hence he became a close and trustworthy friend. Another good friend I met was 'Popps'. He was a West Country boy and, like us, after a short period of time didn't want to be at Stonehouse. Due to the Corps drafting system, he had overstayed his welcome at 42 Commando and been sent to RM Plymouth to work on the provost staff. A big problem with the Corps drafting system was they had an irritating habit of moving happy and well-trained individuals – and there was nothing worse than seeing good oppos being moved for no apparent reason.

Due to Stonehouse's close proximity to Union Street (with its door-to-door pubs and clubs), I decided to make the most of my bad draft decision. With the few single lads on camp we got into a routine of dressing up in silly outfits to go out for the night (a silly rigs run). This ranged from dressing up in trench coats all handcuffed together to wearing babies' nappies. Anything went; the crazier the better.

Life in the dog section became cushy but mundane. We were located in an old fort overlooking Plymouth Sound and away from the hustle and bustle of the main camp. The dogs themselves were loveable animals but the Army's cast-offs. They were hard to keep on top of when it came to training. The obedience, bite and aggression training were enjoyable but made difficult because of the dogs we had: three German shepherds, a Rottweiler and a Dobermann.

After the first few months I put in for a draft back to a Commando unit. The pace of life was slow in the section and most of the Marines were a good bunch but well-served and looking for an easy time for a while.

I also started volunteering for tasks to get involved in activities and away from the prosaic dog section duties.

One evening a number of us, including a sergeant, escorted the local Marine cadets to a disused fort I had visited during my Commando training. We were to play the enemy for a corporals' course. Everything was done as tactically as possible and the kids loved it.

As planned, we soon came under attack. Wally and I attempted to keep events under control, throwing pyrotechnics as an aid to the firefight. The fort and our position were in total darkness and the only things which could be seen were the muzzle flashes from the corporals' weapons.

The events that followed were either fluke or the cadet responsible was very switched on. Either way, the corporals were unaware at the time how close to death and bloodshed they had come. During the blank firing attack, the cadet had noticed the rounds he was loading into his magazine looked like live rounds. Thinking it wasn't possible, he carried on until the moment when he loaded one particular magazine into his SLR. Fumbling in the dark, it felt heavier than the previous ones. To his ever-lasting credit he decided to act on his doubt and ask me. I instantly saw the live rounds in the magazine and assumed at once that others could have some as well. I screamed to stop firing and shouted towards the sergeant. We eventually detected that other live rounds had been mixed into the blank rounds, and traced the problem back to the magazine at camp. The attack was cancelled and the remainder of the night was spent trying to warn other exercises of the potential life-threatening error in case they had fired live rounds by mistake.

My eagerness to get away from the dog section with Wally got us selected to shoot in the unit team. This involved training for two weeks with the SA80 and 9mm Browning pistol. The annual competition for the whole Commando Brigade was held at Hythe ranges in Kent.

We went shooting every day as the CO had given us two weeks to get ready running up to the competition. Fortunately Sergeant Graham, who had been with me during the ammunition incident was in charge, ably assisted by a good friend of mine, Corporal George Craddock, who I had served with at Lympstone and 40 Commando. He was a very experienced weapons instructor approaching the age of retiring, and a dry, very funny man who didn't suffer fools gladly. I enjoyed working with him immensely.

Four Marines were in the team: Wally, Danny, Sam and myself.

Danny was a Lancashire lad from the Chorley area and worked on the provost staff at Stonehouse. I knew very little about Sam, other than that he worked at Brigade Headquarters in Plymouth as a signaller.

The training turned out to be a welcome break from the dog section. My shooting skills developed no end and the work on the range was relaxed to say the least. The sun was also out for most of the two weeks, which was an added bonus, especially on the Dartmoor ranges.

At the competition, the main SA80 rifle shooting didn't go particularly well; we all dropped a few shots. The pistol shooting was completely different. We were all good but Sam was a cracking shot. This didn't ease the nerves as any dropped shot could mean the difference between winning or losing. Once all our 40 rounds had been fired at the various targets, we held our breath for the outcome.

We had won the 1988 McCarthy Cup! And the CO was delighted.

During the summer that followed I received a call from my elder brother asking if I wanted to go on holiday to Magalluf in Majorca. I wasn't that keen, but decided if I could sell my car and raise the cash I would go.

By the end of the week I had sold it and booked a place on the flight. Before setting off, I received my draft preference; I was going to 42 Commando in a few months.

I decided to make the most of the holiday, but little did I know it was going to change my whole life.

Landing in the resort, five of us dumped our belongings and went straight out. I ended up being carried back to my apartment, thus reducing the chance of attracting the opposite sex. I had never had a long-term girlfriend. Most of my relationships had been brief encounters on leave, which lasted only a few weeks. The lifestyle of a travelling Marine Commando did nothing to encourage relationships.

The first few days of the holiday were uneventful but on one particular evening, across a bar I bumped into Mel. She was a trainee nurse from Salford, on holiday with her friends, and we hit it off from the start. Having a long-term relationship couldn't have been further from my mind, yet we kept meeting and ended up spending evenings together without really having to plan it.

As always, the lads joked about the holiday romance and I thought it might turn into one. On my return to England we arranged to meet. We hit it off again. I started to fall in love. Suddenly my burning ambition towards the Corps started to grow dimmer and dimmer. We spent every bit of free time together, and I was able to organise my duties at the dog section to accommodate the time off and travel to Manchester.

This was too good to last because my draft to 42 Commando had arrived and a tour of Northern Ireland was looming. I thought the relationship with Mel would fade if I went because of the time I would have to spend away.

I didn't want this to happen. Mel and I seemed happy together. She even drove down to Plymouth to visit me when I had minor hospital surgery.

Arriving at 42 Commando, I joined M Company. I didn't want to be there. I had grown older and the lads in the company seemed younger. The wind in my sails to be a Commando had vanished. I can't explain why. But I wasn't enjoying the field exercises because my mind was elsewhere with Mel. I had to get away from 42 Commando and

159

fortunately a lad in the company wanted to swap a draft to RM Poole. I rushed to the sergeant major's office and told him I wanted out of the unit. He looked at me in disbelief but I didn't care.

I got my request and moved to Poole. Once there, I started work with the camp provost staff. Within the week I knew I would be leaving the Marines. But what could I do? I had little in the way of qualifications. The Police seemed like a good career: security, no travel and mixed with excitement.

I decided to make the most of the Corps and applied for an education course in GCSE English and maths. At the same time the Corps was also advertising for the Marine Police drafts back to Stonehouse Barracks. That was it, I was going to improve my maths and English and apply for the Corps Police.

I spent very little time at Poole and soon moved back to Stonehouse barracks to begin my Royal Marines Police course.

The Royal Marines Police troop was responsible for administering discipline within the Corps whilst at home and abroad. It was also responsible for route signing the major roads during exercises. I was now at the dizzy height of lance corporal, but I had lost the motivation for promotion. I had never been one to play the system and utter the right phrases.

The RMP course consisted of communications work back at Lympstone. I found it rather strange going back as a trained rank, and a nervous pit formed in my stomach as I drove into the camp. It was a very false environment. A lot of the instructors at Lympstone thought they were gods due to the respect given to them by the nods.

From Lympstone the course took me back to Poole for the driving phase. Passing my bike test, I was sent back to Stonehouse whilst the non-drivers took their full driving tests. This was a great advantage for me as I used the weekend to visit Mel. Back in Plymouth, I found myself on a medics course, working in the operating theatres of the Royal Naval Hospital, learning how to pass ET tubes and monitor people's vital signs. The course opened my eyes to the skills of surgeons and anaesthetists.

At the end I met up with the RM Police course at the Army's Military Police camp in Chichester. The law input on military discipline was fine but the remainder of the course was like pulling teeth. The Army had a completely different way of doing things and had a very bad habit of shouting about it. I was a firm believer in earning people's respect rather than imposing oneself on another.

On passing the course, all eight of us headed back to Plymouth, where we began operational work as Marine Police. This involved a lot of work in the town picking up drunken and foolish Marines. The Marine Police had a little stigma attached to it by the rest of the Corps.

Having spent a lot of time myself getting drunk in Plymouth, I spent more time attempting to get drunken Marines out of the shit. The ones I couldn't help only had themselves to blame.

By now Mel and I had decided to get married, which at 20 years of age was a complete shock to our parents. I still had a contract to serve out, and the trips that went with it.

These included one to the Lake District in winter to conduct mountain training. The weather was extremely bad during the week and river crossings were far from pleasant.

161

But it kept my fitness up and, in a funny way, I enjoyed all the yomping, climbing and route planning. Above all, when there was the odd break in the clouds the scenery was breathtaking.

I was still spending a lot of time away from Mel but we remained in touch via the telephone.

Before long I was on a ski instructors' (MSIs') course in Norway. At the start of the Norwegian winter the snowfall had been rather light for the time of year.

The course was very relaxed and my instructor was an old and jolly Norwegian. He was a real gentleman and an excellent skier on his cross-country planks. We stayed at a private ski lodge, which was very nice compared with the other places I had stayed in. It was a long skiing holiday courtesy of the Marines and I had enjoyed every minute of it – except the last two days.

On the final Sunday morning prior to our tests, four of us left the ski lodge in Atna and began walking up the nearby mountain. The plan for the day was to carry our cross-country skis to the top and then use them to ski back down.

The weather was overcast when we reached the top and we set off full of vigour and excitement. After a short while we all traversed a set of whoops and bumps. This proved to be great fun so we decided to walk back up to go over them again.

Setting off a second time, I followed the same set of tracks as the leader, but getting half way down the whoops and bumps got the better of me. Flipping backwards, my legs shot into the air. I landed on my backside with a chilling bone-breaking snap. Burning sensations raced along my spine and in a panic I tried to move my feet. For a horrible moment I thought I had broken my back on the protruding rock. I couldn't move because of the pain but the three lads

I was with soon got to me. At once they realised how badly injured I was. Two of them quickly left to summon help from the lodge, whilst Tony remained with me. I had known Tony on and off for a few years although we had never served in the same unit together.

After a while, as darkness rapidly approached I started to get very cold. Drifting in and out of consciousness in a sleeping bag, I became aware of my colleagues charging towards me. Fortunately, a few mountain leaders were on the course and they soon had me in a Yelper sledge and back down the mountain. I was whisked off to hospital to discover I had a broken pelvis. That was the end of my ski instructors' course.

However, a few months later and fully recovered, I soon found myself back in Norway on yet another winter deployment.

The beginning and endings of the deployments were always a busy time for the police troop. Lots of men and equipment needed to be moved from ship to shore. This meant a few cold days standing around at the docks unloading ships. It was totally demoralising in the cold wet conditions. I spent most of the remaining months of the deployment at Gardermoen Airfield.

The facilities there were basic, even involving a walk outside in −20° in a towel and flip-flops to the shower block. Getting to the showers was one thing but on occasions the water wasn't even warm, which made the sprint back even quicker.

During our time in Norway we were given tasks to carry out. One was the preparation of a lecture for the remainder of the troop. On a cold snowy morning I was taken to an isolated wood. Alighting from the Land Rover, I saw a concrete memorial on a grassed area. As my boots crunched into the freshly fallen snow, I noticed how quiet and eerie the place was. The Tradum Memorial was dedicated to the lives of 173 Norwegians, 15 Soviets and 6 British who had been murdered in the wood by the Germans during 1940 and 1945.

A track led through the woods to a number of stone crosses, which indicated where the victims had fallen. Walking around the wood, I thought how they must have felt walking to their deaths in this cold and isolated place. Fear, apprehension, panic, terror, and anxiety must have been only a few of the emotions racing around their frightened minds. Why had it happened? Who could have *let* it happen?

I returned for a remembrance service a few days later and was so struck by the place I decided to research the history and present my lecture on the isolated and forgotten graveyard.

The deployment seemed to drag on and on, but whilst I was away from England Mel was making our wedding plans and I was counting down the days. During the trip I had decided enough was enough and paid to leave the Corps. My whole attitude had changed because of my encounter with Mel in Spain 15 months earlier.

Back in England having sailed through the beautiful Norwegian fjords, I was suddenly facing wedding nerves.

7

DOING IT FOR REAL

Mel and I had finally found time to honeymoon and the Corps seemed a million miles away, especially now we were visiting the sights of Los Angeles, California.

We were staying with my aunt close to Disneyland in Orange County and life was extremely relaxing. That was, until one morning, eating breakfast, I caught sight of the latest CNN news report.

Saddam Hussein, dictator of Iraq, had ordered his troops to invade Kuwait. The small defence force of Kuwait had made brave attempts to slow the mighty Republican Guard as it surged towards the capital, but news coverage showed tanks steamrolling into Kuwait City.

The newsreaders discussed the aftermath and the political implications of why it had all happened.

Mel sensed my attention had become focused on the TV. She sat quietly for a moment taking it all in, then turned to me and said, 'Oh my God, that's not good news.'

Chewing on a mouthful of breakfast, I replied, 'Don't be stupid,' hoping she would switch off and ignore the obsessive press attention.

Attempting to put the conflict at the back of my mind, I carried on with our fantastic holiday. The sights and sounds around LA, Vegas and the Grand Canyon were to remain with me until this day. But, like all holidays, it soon came to an end.

Back in Plymouth, I endeavoured to settle down to married life. However, rumours started circulating about being sent to the Gulf. It was quickly becoming obvious from the British television coverage that the West wouldn't take long to protect its oil interests in the Middle East.

The US government was the first to react and rapidly began sending men and equipment to the region. The British government quickly followed and soon a large coalition force had amassed in the Middle East, with the Saudis playing host to the majority of the coalition.

I tried hard not to think about it and made an extra effort to ease Mel's concerns. Being sent to the Gulf was the last thing I wanted. I was studying vigorously for a GCSE in English to improve my education, in the hope that this would increase my chances of getting into the Police.

Work was more or less the same but the brigade on the whole was preparing itself for the big call-up. Kit and vehicles were being checked and serviced. The local newspaper, *The Evening Herald*, was printing various bulletins about the local Marine units. Everybody was awaiting the call to the region.

Early in the morning of 17th January 1991 I was getting ready for work when I switched on the radio.

The war had begun.

Every TV and radio programme was crammed with facts about how Operation Desert Storm had started. Wave after wave of air strikes had been directed at Iraq and targets in occupied Kuwait. The raids included bombing strikes by RAF Tornados, US Stealth Bombers and Tomahawk cruise missiles.

I couldn't believe it. For a moment life began to repeat

itself. All I kept thinking about was how similar the news was to when the Falklands War had begun so many years previously.

The only difference now was that I was trained to do the job. I somehow felt jealous of not being part of it. Was I failing in my ambition of becoming involved in active service?

It was a very strange day indeed. Most of it was spent close to a television set, talking with oppos and discussing various scenarios that included our involvement.

I wasn't the only person to be affected by the Gulf. Mel had also been placed on a war footing. Being a nurse on the regional burns ward she had been told to expect casualties from the war. In fact, everyone in Plymouth was affected by it in some way.

Days passed quickly during the war and before long the allies had announced a cease-fire. Was this right? Many people seemed to ask this question. But the TV had the biggest effect on public opinion, especially when civilian casualties were shown at peak-time viewing.

My thoughts quickly returned to my pending return to civilian life in six months. I had passed my Police entrance exam along with my 'B' grade GCSE English. The Gulf War seemed to be fading away day by day into another historical event that I had missed.

However, the allies had failed to recognise the false promises they had given to the people of Iraq during Operation Desert Storm. The Kurds in Northern Iraq had taken the allies at their word and attempted to revolt against their dictator, Saddam Hussein. As a result of this unsupported uprising, Saddam Hussein had unleashed his troops into Northern Iraq in an attempt to quell the revolts and retain his grip on power.

The ensuing one-sided bloody conflict resulted in tens of thousands of people fleeing their homes into the surrounding mountains. This in turn caused a major refugee crisis. Children and the elderly started dying from the harsh winter conditions and lack of food.

Again, the news coverage created another problem for the politicians. They had to do something, and fast. So they decided to send the Marines.

Unaware of this decision, Mel and I had taken to the road and were travelling back to Manchester in order to attend her best friend's wedding. It was a Thursday and I had been given leave until Monday.

We arrived, looking forward to the day when Alison finally tied the knot. Walking through the door of Mel's mum's house the happiness suddenly turned to shock.

She greeted us with the remark, 'Haven't you heard the news? They're sending the Marines to Iraq.'

Mel appeared dazed by this. I couldn't seem to grasp the idea that I might be going to the Gulf. I had this notion in my mind that the politicians would change their minds before any deployments were made.

Then the telephone rang. Instinctively I already knew who it was. Picking up the receiver and saying 'Hello', I was met by a distinctive voice.

'It's the sergeant major here.'

'All right, sir, I've heard the news.'

'OK, stay for the wedding, but be back by Sunday.'

'Thanks very much, sir.'

'Don't forget your kit as I want you ready to go by Monday morning.'

'OK, no problem.'

Putting the receiver down, I reflected on the conversation and what it meant.

I was going to a warzone!

This wasn't supposed to be happening. I had only just got married and was planning to leave the Corps for a new life.

Why now? Why couldn't it have happened five years ago when I was chomping at the bit to get stuck in? Now I was becoming de-mob happy with the thought of starting a new career in the Police.

Overnight I was being thrust into a direction I didn't wish to travel. For the first time in my life I was now feeling the true whip of being in the armed forces and deploying on active service. Uncertainty, loneliness and fear were only a few of the emotions spinning around my mind.

The only solution I had was to make the most of my final days in the UK. So out I went. Sometimes life seemed better staring at it through the bottom of a pint pot.

Many hours later and still rather intoxicated I found myself staggering home behind Mel and friends. Then suddenly I was brought back to reality with a semi-sobered mind when I heard Mel's panic-stricken voice.

'Where's the car? Where's the car?' she kept shouting.

Looking at the spot where I had parked the car when we had arrived, I saw a vacant space.

Fuck me, I thought. I had enough on my mind. The last thing I wanted to do was chase around Manchester in an attempt to find our stolen car. But how was I going to get back to Plymouth with Mel?

I couldn't believe that some spotty-faced, bone-idle teenager had nicked my car. I was boiling with rage. I was close to the point of exploding and losing all my self-control. I prayed that I would find the scrote responsible. The only justice he could have received was a good thrashing. Probation and community work was nonsense. Harsh treatment worked in the Marines and had been tested in the Forces for decades. It had taught people right across society how to respect and appreciate things in life.

Calming down, I contacted the local police. Within a couple of hours, having been chased and crashed into someone's front garden, it was recovered and brought back to Mel's house. But I soon realised it would never make the journey back to Plymouth.

Thinking I had dreamt the whole event, I was awoken on Friday morning by yet another phone call.

This time, it wasn't so welcoming.

I was told the day for the move off had been brought forward and I needed to be back in Plymouth by Saturday morning. Upon hearing this news, Mel instantly broke into tears. She was going to miss her best friend's wedding, the car had been smashed up, I was going to Iraq on my return and we had to get back to Plymouth somehow.

Fortunately, the AA agreed to take us back to Plymouth along with the car.

The farewells from Manchester were very sad for us all. Doubt about the future had spread into all of our minds.

The journey back to Plymouth took an epic 12 hours and was extremely taxing on our patience.

Back in our cosy home, I started to sort my kit out, only to discover that the planned departure date had been set back until further notice. Hurry up and wait was something I had grown accustomed to in the Corps. Mel hadn't, and was angry to say the least when the time for my departure was put back. I was now on standby whilst other parts of the brigade set off for Turkey.

The ensuing week proved to be extremely painful for Mel, not knowing whether I was staying or going. Every day had a shadow of doubt cast over it, especially when Mel left for work. We treated every goodbye as the final goodbye before I left.

The problem of not having a car had temporarily been solved by having borrowed a friend's clapped-out Escort. It had no credibility but did the job of getting Mel to work at Derriford Hospital on time.

One morning that week while Mel was at work, I had a home visit from the local police inspector. This was due to my success in passing the Police entrance exam. I didn't know what to expect, but the informal visit was relaxed and he took his time to ask various questions about my family. I had the impression he seemed interested in what I had to say, bearing in mind I was applying to Greater Manchester Police and not his force, Devon and Cornwall.

Settling into the conversation and putting what nerves I had behind me, I received the expected telephone call. One of the lads from the troop informed me that I was required back at camp ASAP. I cut the inspector short and told him I was required for deployment.

He completely understood my predicament and said, 'Well, the car's outside. I'll give you a lift!'

Grabbing what stuff I had at home, I made my way to Stonehouse Barracks.

My police application was now on hold, but the inspector confirmed he would let the relevant people know where I was and that I wasn't able to make contact.

My vehicle and equipment had been ready for days, so I took the opportunity to call for our final farewell. Mel's voice seemed strained with emotion and I felt inconsolable, thinking how much I was going to miss her.

What could I say to her? I didn't have a clue what was going to happen next. Mel was far too clever to be fooled by my bullshit about how quickly I would be returning. Nobody, including politicians, had any idea how the Kurdish crisis was going to be solved. What would happen if the Iraqi troops didn't want to withdraw from Northern Iraq? Would it mean fighting? If so, it was something I was going to have to come to terms with, and quickly.

The briefing outlined the phases for the move from Plymouth to RAF Lyneham. Then the four-Land-Rover convoy I was travelling in, containing two Marines in each vehicle, set off from Plymouth.

As we were driving along the motorway my mind began to wander again. I watched every vehicle that raced past on the outside lane of the A38. The drivers and passengers seemed completely oblivious to my presence on the road. Here I was driving to a possible conflict and they were out on an afternoon drive to Tesco or on a trip home from work to spend time with their families.

I began to realise that I had made the right decision to leave the Marines. Nobody, especially fellow countrymen and women, seemed to care. Here I was prepared to lay down my life for so-called democracy. Car after car raced by, the occupants seemingly more worried about why I was holding them up than where I was going.

I had become so different in the last five years. I had grown from an insignificant, immature young boy to somebody filled with confidence and self-respect who was prepared to question others. I was confident in making decisions, and someone who could be expected to get on with a job when asked.

Arriving at RAF Lyneham, I was ordered from one place to the next until finally we were loading our vehicle onto the back of a C130 Hercules.

Not long after this, I was airborne, watching England disappear through a small fuselage window. Even with foam ear defenders, the noise from the engines was deafening.

After a short while the aircrew gave me the thumbs-up, so I undid my seat belt, clambered aboard the roof of the Land Rover, got my sleeping bag out and attempted to get some sleep. God only knew when I'd be getting any more.

Having spent a refuelling stop in Italy, I was awoken to say we would shortly be arriving at an airbase in southern Turkey.

As the C130 approached the airfield, nerves tingled through my body in anticipation. I felt strange, as if I was in a dream. I couldn't believe that in less than 24 hours I had travelled half way around the world.

From the warm living-room of my house discussing a future in the Police, I was now on the verge of entering one of the most potentially hostile places in the world.

Driving down the rear ramp of the Hercules, I was surprised to discover how humid and damp the climate was. The airfield seemed to be a hive of activity. Vehicles from many countries were heading in all directions and Turkish fighter planes were landing and taking off in pairs. It felt as if I was driving onto the *MASH* film set.

The surrounding countryside seemed so green, with lush vegetation in abundance around the runway. The adjacent fields were thick with muddy tyre tracks caused by the sudden influx of vehicles.

Pulling away from the sanctuary of the aircraft, I was directed by Turkish marshals to the side of the airfield.

As I drove towards this quagmire, I began to recognise a number of other vehicles from my unit. I soon discovered they had been waiting hours in this location. The majority of the lads had been given no indication of when they would be setting off.

Thinking I was going to be at the airfield for a long while, I made an attempt to get myself comfortable. To my surprise, we had been the last vehicles they had all been waiting for. Without warning, we began to move off. It turned out that the delay had been caused by the Turkish authorities complaining about the amount of mud being driven onto their roads.

Any sort of briefing for the journey went straight out of the window and it quickly became something like the wacky racers cartoon that I used to watch as a child.

When we set off from the airfield, civilian traffic was fairly minimal, but the abundance of military vehicles soon became apparent. Instinctively, I just followed the vehicle in front; I had no idea where we were heading.

Pausing at a nearby junction, I seized the chance to stop and ask another Marine where the hell we were supposed to be heading.

Turning his dust-covered face towards me he replied, 'Follow the signs to Salopi, mate!'

'Where the fuck's Salopi?' I shouted as we drove past. All he could manage in reply was a dry smile and a shrug of his shoulders.

Great, I thought. I had no map, no idea where we were or how far we were going. It really was a shambles.

Fortunately, I wasn't alone in my Land Rover. I was accompanied by Ady, who was travelling to the brigade HQ with me. I had never met him before but the long journey from Plymouth had enabled us to get to know each other.

The only problem was that when I did eventually ask him to take a turn of the driving he informed me that he didn't hold a current British driving licence. Fortunately that wasn't going to stop him, because we were now in Turkey and nobody seemed to give a shit!

I couldn't believe how poorly organised everything seemed to be. Nobody was getting a grip of the situation. Years of training just ebbed into insignificance. When I finally did manage to get my hands on a map I soon realised that Salopi was hundreds of miles away. I didn't even have a clue where we were going to refuel.

Mile after mile we progressed along poor-quality roads covered in potholes. Slowly but surely vehicles began to break down and our snake of vehicles left a wake of unserviceable stragglers as we raced south towards Salopi.

The flat barren land soon gave way to rocky mountains, putting even more stress on our overladen vehicles. We were now in what appeared to be a very isolated part of Turkey. Daylight rapidly began to change into darkness, adding to my concerns about where we were heading. Fuel from the two petrol tanks was also getting low and the signposts for Salopi were rare, to say the least.

With the needle on the red line and many hours into the next day, we eventually arrived at the outskirts of Salopi. It was now extremely dark and dangerous. Vehicles, including huge HGVs, were travelling at night without any lights on. The main road south into Salopi was nose to tail with lorries awaiting confirmation to enter Iraq with supplies.

Americans seemed to be everywhere, but well-organised. I, on the other hand, had no idea where our troop location was. Fortunately, after lots of confusion, in the middle of a cornfield we finally found where the remainder of the troop were. The sergeant major and the lads came out to meet us.

Over the preceding months and during the build-up to our deployment we had all become good friends. When you are many miles from home a familiar face is the next best thing to home.

Dumping my kit into a free tent I snatched some rest before the proper work began.

Next day started bright and early. The morning sunshine soon revealed that the brigade headquarters was a massive network of tents and makeshift dirt roads. Our particular position occupied a knee-high wheat field which was still drying out from recent rain.

Rushing breakfast, I washed my already grimy body and waited for the next briefing. In this period I was handed extra rifle magazines and ammunition. Some of the lads had already spent a number of days in this location and described the local set-up. The general consensus was that if you needed anything, from food to fuel, you went to see the Americans.

Looking directly south from our position, I could see the mountains of Northern Iraq. At their foot was the border crossing, which Turkish soldiers manned, that was to be our main entry point into Iraq.

Some 2,000 metres south-west of our position inside Turkey was a newly constructed refugee camp, surrounded by a ten-foot concrete wall. Inside the perimeter were row after row of canvas tents containing thousands of Kurdish refugees. The wall prevented anybody from escaping, and also stopped straying eyes looking in.

It immediately struck me as a potential epidemic factory due to its lack of sanitation. Only time would tell.

Directly to the north was the town of Salopi. This was a typical border town, which at first sight seemed to have little or no individual character. The streets were a mass of modern-day motor vehicles combined with donkeys and carts from years gone by. Bedraggled, dirty beige-coloured shop fronts bore all the trademarks of Western ways, each displaying its wares to passing trade. There was a distinct lack of individualism, with every shop appearing to sell the same type of goods as the next one. American dollars were more welcome than the local currency, which said a lot about the local economy.

Salopi was a very busy place during the day but there always seemed to be a noticeable presence of Turkish soldiers. When darkness fell the realities of the local problems soon became quite apparent. Southern Turkey, including the town of Salopi, had once been part of Kurdistan. Since then the local PKK (Kurdish Workers Party) had been in dispute with Turkey over its right for independence. But, as with our own problems in Northern Ireland, certain factions had decided to take up arms for their cause. This resulted in regular terrorist operations against Turkish military units and other government targets.

After we had settled into our new environment, the sergeant major instructed us to mount a two-vehicle patrol into Iraq and visit the town of Zakho. The aim of the patrol was to check the main supply route into the country and ascertain if the brigade's HGVS would be safe to travel to the various supply points set up by the forward units of the coalition force.

This was it. It wasn't training any longer. God was the only one who knew what was going to happen when we crossed the border!

I kept checking my kit again and again. The briefing was very short and to the point. We all knew our jobs but had no idea what to expect. Because of the political situation, we had been instructed to fire only if fired upon.

Climbing aboard our open-top Land Rovers, we set off heading south towards the border.

Travelling past the refugee camp, I could see over the wall. Clothes were hung out in every available space but the place seemed to be devoid of people. There was a very cold and isolated feeling in the air. Momentarily, a shiver made its way down my spine.

When we reached the isolated border post, the large vehicle reception area was deserted. Many of the buildings bore the scars of conflict. Damaged bricks and small circular pits in concrete were pebble-dashed everywhere the eye could see. Sullen-looking border guards occupied a number of the checkpoints. They seemed to be disillusioned with their lives, but months and months in this lonely outpost would have destroyed anybody's morale and motivation.

Eventually, after some heated discussion, we were given access across the border. Travelling over the river Khabur, we drove onto Iraqi soil.

The adjacent Iraqi border position was empty of any signs of life. It was just like a ghost town in a spaghetti western, with grass and debris being blown across the tarmac in the breeze.

Racing through the unmanned crossing, we quickly joined the main road that took us towards Zakho. A short distance separated our vehicles in order to give us time to react to any potential danger. The familiar whining sound of the tyres was now an ever-present background noise. Each Land Rover contained three Marines. I was travelling in the second vehicle in a standing position, ready to react if fired upon.

Adrenaline was gushing through my apprehensive body. I had no idea what was going to happen so I tried to be ready for anything. I rapidly surveyed the surrounding ground, picking out threats and potential trouble spots. I feared a well-orchestrated ambush. Mountains lined the road to the right, with the river and open ground to the left. A number of destroyed Soviet-built tanks were intermittently deployed around the edge of the mountains, but again there was no evidence of any Iraqi troop movement.

At the edge of Zakho, the sight that greeted us etched itself into my memory.

Children in rags were playing in the gutters and drains at the roadside. Many were covered in open sores with scabs and flies all over them, disfiguring their once beautiful little faces. One little girl's entire mouth was thick with flies. She had apparently grown tired and weary of brushing them away as she made no sign of being aware of them. She was standing in a dishevelled blue dress covered in dry mud. Her hair, which had plainly not seen water in weeks, was matted with dirt and dust from the passing vehicles. Her large brown innocent eyes looked up at our Land Rover as we drove slowly past.

Thankful for what she had received from us in the way of boiled sweets from our rations, she clutched at the packet as if her life depended on it. But the most frightening fact of all was that she also clasped an anti-personnel mine in her other hand, totally unaware of the danger it contained. This was her own little bargaining tool. As a child at home would cling to a dolly, she clung to the mine in the same caring way, hoping that we would trade some of our own food for it.

I could feel myself becoming as terrified as she was. I had no idea if it was live or defused. Then, to my horror, children began running towards us in their droves. Every other boy or girl seemed to possess some kind of war trophy: RPG rocket heads, startling arrays of anti-personnel mines, AK-47 assault rifle bayonets and assortments of ammunition. This sight was terrifying mainly because they were unaware of all the dangers around them. And I knew exactly what they were.

We had no option but to get the hell out. So we quickly accelerated towards the town occupied by the coalition and Kurdish rebels.

Reaching the town, we came to our first major junction, which led us into the centre. Lots more people were walking the streets but thankfully they paid less attention to us. Kurdish men sat outside shanty-style cafés, while the women seemed to be trying to get life back to normal.

Every other building was destroyed. Stopping to speak to some locals in pidgin English, I soon found out why. When the Iraqis had withdrawn from the area prior to the coalition's arrival they had systematically blown up all the main buildings, leaving a trail of destruction. All sanitation systems had been destroyed. Electrical installations and any kind of industry had been wrecked.

Eventually we reached the forward detachment and re-supplied them with food and water. A couple of the lads had started to look fatigued, so they were allowed back to Salopi for a day for a wash and rest. This particular day was very demanding travelling around Zakho. Eventually, having run the gauntlet of the children many times, we crossed back into Turkey.

180

The overall plan was to move the brigade east through Batufa and set up another HQ inside Iraq at Sirsenk Airport, where there was a partly-constructed airfield.

Day by day we travelled further and further into Iraq.

One morning we were instructed to set up a forward checkpoint at Batufa. The Dutch Marines occupied this location but our role was to check the flow of brigade's traffic through the town. Fortunately, I was going to be accompanied by William, Lester and Davies.

As time passed, the border crossings became less and less daunting. Even the children outside Zakho were less intimidating and I had grown used to stopping and speaking to them, even though they held deadly weapons.

Our checkpoint was on the east side of Batufa, at the side of a large, featureless mountain. At its summit was an old fort, which we avoided at all costs in case it had been booby-trapped by the withdrawing Iraqis. The town was very small but many of its inhabitants had recently returned from the mountains. Whilst sorting our equipment out I took in the passing dishevelled-looking locals. Some would stop and stare at us. Others, especially the children, would stay for hours, watching our every move.

Aware that we were now very isolated, we got ourselves into a routine.

Communications had to be established with our troop HQ back in Salopi. This proved to be difficult because of the large mountain between our location and the general direction of brigade HQ in Turkey. Two of us were required to climb up this mountain and construct the radio mast.

I began the climb with Davies, but as ever I soon started thinking about landmines. I hadn't ventured far off the main roads, so this was my first stroll onto a terrain covered in mines. Every step I took was mentally painful; I hoped it wasn't going to be me who got his foot blown off. Mines, mines, mines. The designers knew exactly how to prey upon one's mind.

The sooner I got up, the sooner I could return to the relative safety of our checkpoint. At the top I had my first opportunity to view the town. The surrounding countryside was beautiful: green vegetation and mountains made it picturesque. For a few brief seconds I dreamt that I wasn't in this godforsaken place.

Getting down to the bottom and feeling excitedly safe, I suddenly dived to the ground. A massive explosion ripped into the silent air, causing my heart to miss a beat. Realising I wasn't in any harm, I looked at William, who smiled, and said, 'What the fuck's going on?'

Lester was already laughing, and I soon discovered that the Dutch Marines had just blown up a large pile of found munitions.

'Thanks for the fucking warnings,' I said as I joined in the laughter.

Our checkpoint now had to be manned 24 hours a day, but because of the lack of communications we decided to double up. This meant working every 12 hours.

I got the first watch with William. As the night started to draw in, fires began to appear in the houses and tents occupied by the frightened Kurds. The position was very isolated and lonely, making us feel vulnerable. Wild domestic dogs ran around in packs. They were invisible to the naked eye but the barks got nearer as they ventured closer to us. Our night sights allowed us to see them and direct the odd stone to fend them off.

Towards the early hours, William and I began to talk the

night away: how long we reckoned the operation would last, runs ashore, life's experiences, friends, families and sport. The topics were endless. A lot of the time was talking about home – William was planning to leave the Corps, like me. He was a physically fit Scotsman and a proficient corporal who was probably one of the best oppos I was ever going to have in the Corps. Our backgrounds were totally different. He was married and in the final stages of being accepted by the Australian Army. The funny thing about our situation that night was that we really didn't want to be in Iraq!

The next day children began to notice our new checkpoint. We seemed totally strange to them, like an alien force that had appeared from space. They watched every move we made. Did they regard us as saints, freedom fighters, saviours, friends or foes? Not one of them could tell us. Since I didn't have any children, my contact and experience with them was limited, I couldn't even estimate their ages.

The lads in the detachment tried to make them feel welcome by giving them the sweets from our rations. Every day the same group of boys would return. One particular child was obviously excluded from the group because he was mentally ill. The other children seemed to view him as a threat. The ceremony of handing out boiled sweets whipped the kids into frenzy. Every time this boy approached us the others began to slap and hit him. If this vicious behaviour didn't deter him, they would begin to stone the poor lad. It was barbaric and at times painful to watch as the dull thuds echoed off his fragile body. The treatment handed out from the other boys was so disturbing that we often had to intervene.

The odd thing was that they all seemed so happy to be close to us. They paid little or no attention to the weapons we were carrying and were totally unconcerned by their surroundings of burnt-out and destroyed buildings.

Before long the ritual of moving forward continued and we were heading past Sarsenk airport.

In between the stress and strains we did find time to laugh and joke. One place we occupied was a disused petrol station on the main road into Dahook, where the Pesh-merger guerillas helped us monitor the influx of people in and out of the safe haven as they wanted to find Iraqi police whom they suspected of surveying the coalition forces.

The petrol station itself provided no shelter because the Iraqis had left excrement everywhere inside the buildings, making it uninhabitable for us. We set up a position outside and decided to use the old underground petrol tanks as a toilet. A makeshift seat gave us a little extra comfort whilst breathing in the petrol vapours.

Nobody thought anything of it until we came to move location again. Marty, who was a typical Mancunian and of Arthur Daly character, decided to throw a lighted cigarette into the tank. A few lads had gathered around as Marty had made common knowledge of his intentions.

It was a sight to savour. The flame from the tank exploded 30 feet into the air, knocking him off his feet. The compression and heat also disbursed a fine mist of excrement like a cluster bomb. Fortunately I was outside the blast range but others weren't so lucky. Getting to his feet, Marty was red-faced and rather smelly!

A few months after deploying I started to get fed up with

the daily routine. Intermingled with this, though, were the tragic day-to-day incidents I witnessed.

On a journey back through the mountains we were driving along a rock-covered path that was, allegedly, a road over a ridgeline.

Most of the trucks on the Kurdish roadways were designed originally to carry rubble to and from quarries. The problem was, these had all been adapted to carry people. Coming down the track at a noticeably fast speed was one of these vehicles, containing about 20 guerilla fighters. They were being thrown viciously about as the truck increased its speed, bouncing and vibrating as it went. Then in slow motion it dawned on me that the truck wasn't able to stop. Shouting could be heard from a couple of vehicles which were attempting to follow. Unable to do anything, I watched in horror as the truck bounced down the mountain on its hellish decent. One by one the occupants were catapulted from the vehicle, unable to keep a hold of the truck, which had now turned into a wild horse at a rodeo show.

After a few life-long seconds the truck left the road, flipped onto its side and shed the remainder of its living load. The sound of crashing metal against rocks quickly faded into silence. Then the cries of the seriously injured could be heard. Six or seven bodies lay motionless on the ground, obviously dead. The vehicles following arrived and the area immediately turned into a hive of activity, and bodies which seemed to be moving were thrown into vehicles and hastily driven away.

We stopped to assist but a language barrier met us and the number of people present swallowed up our effort to help. We were not required. Men with serious fractures lay writhing in agony on the ground. There was no 999 system in these mountains and the Kurds seemed to accept this type of accident as a daily occupational hazard.

After giving some of our medical equipment, we continued with our journey as if nothing had happened.

Another such incident was inside Turkey, close to the border point. There was minimal road sense in this part of the world, which was a recipe for bad accidents. This one happened on a straight piece of road that ran for miles between Salopi and the border point. A truck driver carrying fuel was travelling away from the border, when a taxi-type vehicle travelling in the opposite direction went for a crazy overtake. The truck driver had little time to react and both vehicles hit head-on. The explosion and fireball could be seen for miles around. The driver was killed instantly and all we could do was watch as the fire burnt fiercely out of control. I refused to wait and watch the recovery of the body.

After some time the Kurdish people had started to return home to the villages in their thousands, which increased the rumours about going home. I made brief contacts with Mel over the telephone from Turkey and worried constantly about my looming discharge – would I manage to get into the Police?

Every now and then a few rounds fired at night brought me crashing back to reality. Diving for the shell scraps we had dug at every position, I realised what fear was really about. For me the unknown was worse than facing the fear.

At least I had a little good news in that Mel had been offered a nursing post on a Manchester Regional Burns Unit.

But every day was being wished away. I longed increasingly to be back home so I could carry on with my own life. A career in Manchester Police seemed rather attractive; I wouldn't need to pack up my kit every few weeks and leave Mel.

William was also eager to return home for his impending move to Australia.

With the rumours of our departure, the Kurds started mistrusting us. They seemed to believe we were abandoning them, which would allow the Iraqis back into Kurdistan.

All sorts of scenarios started circulating with the rumour wagon. What would happen if the Kurds turned their weapons on us, for instance? Nobody liked to think about it.

But as the trucks from the coalition forces started to withdraw, the Kurds became noticeably more hostile towards us. They began to ignore us at checkpoints and told the children to stay away. The days dragged on and the hostility increased with each departing truck.

Then, finally, I was told that I would be returning home with an advance party. I was going Home! Relief, happiness and impatience were my mixed emotions.

But the happiness was short-lived. A couple of weeks before I was due to depart William and I were using the troop motorbikes to get up to the edge of the safe haven. Descending the treacherous mountain road, I was in front leading the way when we entered another set of sweeping bends. Coming out of the bends onto a welcome straight, I glanced behind me and noticed William was missing. I turned around and retraced the route. He was lying in the road and for a horrible second I thought he was dead. His bike was a tangled mess at the edge of the road. Then to my relief as I got closer he started to move. He scrambled to his feet but gripped his shoulder and stooped like the hunchback of Notre Dame. His face and arms were covered in bad abrasions. I quickly realised he had either broken his shoulder or collarbone. He was also very pale and going into shock. Fuck! I had no radio, and the closest sanctuary was a company from 45 Commando about four or five miles away.

My main concern was to help William get medical attention. I was getting concerned about any internal bleeding because of his cold clammy face. Then, astonishingly and out of the blue, a Kurdish taxi appeared. The two occupants stopped and I beckoned them to assist. They did, and to my relief we managed to get William into their car. We raced towards the nearest unit, leaving William's bike at the roadside. Getting to 45 Commando's forward position, I screamed for the company medic. Before long a few lads were surrounding us and helping William out of the vehicle. He was now in their hands and I could relax a little, and I thanked the Kurds for helping me.

William was soon given gas and air, which had a reverse effect and turned him into a giggling wreck. Although he was in immense pain, the last vision I had of him was sitting up laughing.

Before leaving Iraq I visited him in the field hospital. Although he was in a lot of pain he seemed happy in the knowledge that he would be going home before me.

The day to leave arrived. I was like an excited child on Christmas Day. Some of the lads were threaders (unhappy) that I was going home before them. Their dull expressions were evident when I grabbed my Bergen in haste to get to the Chinook helicopter that was going to fly me back to the Turkish airport.

As always the flight didn't go to plan. The Chinook developed a problem, which caused us to change helicopter. Then once on the plane back to the UK we had to stop overnight in Cyprus owing to another mechanical problem.

On touching down in England, a great relief surged through me. The sights, sounds and smells back in Iraq were distant memories. Walking from the C-130 I saw it was dull, overcast and raining but I didn't give a damn.

Our desert camouflage kit earned us some odd looks when we stopped at the service station near Bristol on the coach journey back to Plymouth. A number of the people in the shop seemed incensed that we had increased the size of the queues, but a couple of old boys from a coach party seemed to recognise who we were and where we had just come from.

Before long we were pulling up at the main gates of Stonehouse Barracks. Nervously getting off the coach, I was met by nobody. Grabbing my Bergen, I walked to the main gates outside the barracks to await Mel's arrival.

Dropping my kit, I said a quick hello to the lads who had remained back at the camp during our deployment. But I felt ill with nerves. I just wanted to see Mel and get to our house. My mind was racing. I wanted a bath and some home comforts, like a sofa and a beer out of the fridge.

Standing waiting for Mel, I began I think about life again. Like the trip a few months earlier when I had set out on this adventure to the Middle East. Nobody really gave a shit. Life was passing me by again. People just walked past as if nothing had been going on. No welcome, nothing. I wanted to tell my story but nobody wanted to listen.

Mel's face was an image I would never forget. God, I had missed her.

8

A CAREER FOR LIFE

Absence had made the heart grow fonder. Mel and I had so much to plan. She would soon be returning to Manchester and a new nursing post. The days spent in Iraq had changed me, but I chose to avoid talking about what I had witnessed. When people asked me what it had been like I found it easier to answer that it was hot and hard work. I didn't feel proud of what I had seen: misery, sadness and the poor innocent children. It seemed better to try and forget.

Back in England, Iraq felt a million miles away. The sensation of coming home from a violent environment and jumping straight into a peaceful one seemed rather peculiar, like a dream or a fascinating adventure. But the pace of ordinary life took over again and I shut the sights out and projected my thoughts towards a new career in the Police.

My application had been accepted and I slowly progressed through the recruitment process. I volunteered to defer my leave and take it before my discharge date, so Mel moved back to Manchester and I moved back into Stonehouse Barracks to await my discharge.

Eventually the day arrived and I had to go before the Commanding Officer to be formally discharged. Standing outside his office, I suddenly started to feel vulnerable and anxious. As I waited, my thoughts went back over the previous six years. I had certainly come a long way. Many events had taken place since I first arrived on the train at Lympstone Station. I had matured into a confident individual who was very determined, responsible and motivated. Along the way I had made many good friends whom I happily trusted with my life – young lads ready to stand for the things they thought were right, as their fellow countrymen had done before them. I had experienced things that many would never get the opportunity to do. I'd learned to work hard and push myself further than I thought was humanly possible. I knew now never to take anything for granted; there had been times when the everyday items in life seemed like a dream. Although I'd experienced many hard and painful times in the Corps, it had been a great time, with memories which would surely last a lifetime.

A couple of us were getting discharged but a few other lads in uniform were standing with us. They were just joining and I sensed them staring at me. They glanced at me intermittently in a way that I had done when I had first joined, clearly thinking, Why are they leaving?

Marching smartly into the Commanding Officer's room, I stood while he began a parrot-fashioned pep talk. He thanked me for my efforts, handed me my testimonial and wished me good luck in Civvy Street.

It was all very false. He didn't even know who I was. I certainly didn't have a clue who he was, having never uttered a word in conversation. Finally the CO and the sergeant major shook my hand. I turned around and was free to go. I was a civvy!

For the first time in my life I felt alone, as if I had just been released from prison. As I walked to the main gate a few oppos came over to wish me luck. I felt subdued, as if I was losing something.

The last person to say farewell was William at the Police

Troop. He had finally recovered from his injury sustained in Iraq and was now planning to stay in the Corps. I knew he would be successful in whatever he decided to do.

Was I making the right decision? I didn't know. Perhaps it was fate. Whatever the reason, I was now entering a new chapter in my life.

I drove out of Plymouth.

The months in Civvy Street passed very quickly. I found it strange living in Manchester because I had no friends to go out with. I felt rather isolated from the many companions I had once had. Being unemployed for six weeks wasn't nice, so it was to my relief I was finally accepted for recruit training with Greater Manchester Police.

Although GMP was another large predominantly uniform organisation, I couldn't believe how laid back it appeared to be. Subconsciously I anticipated the training would be on a par with the Marines but it couldn't have been further from it. It felt as if the penny was about to drop and a deluge of beastings and late nights would ensue. But they never came.

Instead, a totally alien environment met me. The system of self-assessments and character analysis troubled me as it was geared to pick up everyone's weaknesses. People started writing nonsense in their personal development plans just to fill the pages. I was well aware of my strengths and weaknesses and didn't like the wrap-up-everyone-in-cotton-wool attitude.

But I was now a civvy and the quicker I came to terms with this the better it would be for me. Initially I found it difficult working with women and some of the whingeing men. I found myself concentrating hard on what I said in order to not to offend some heightened sensitivities. It all seemed so false.

The law was designed to confuse, and it certainly did this with me. Classroom discussions in the force and the national training establishments went around and around. The lectures were at times immensely boring because of the love of flip charts. Knuckling down, however, I got my head into the books and studied the theory side of the Police.

Thankfully, having been posted to Brownley Road Police Station in South Manchester, it wasn't long before I was out on the streets learning the job. The station covered Wythenshawe, allegedly the largest inner city council estate in Europe. With Moss Side a short drive away, drugs, violence and all the associated crime were all too common. I felt better being away from the classroom because I was able to use common-sense. The discussions on law and procedure were easy to comprehend in a nice cosy classroom environment; it was completely different under pressure on the streets of inner city Manchester. In my opinion the codes of practice which governed Police powers were good in theory but in truth it tied an arm behind our backs in the battle against crime.

My two tutor constables, Stan and Jim, were completely different characters. Stan was a real up-and-at-you cop, which was very good when dealing with violent and abusive individuals. Some of the scrotes I came into contact with had little respect for themselves, let alone anyone else. Stan brought them into line on many occasions with his speak-how-it-is attitude.

Jim, on the other hand, was a jolly intelligent man who was able to digest problems very quickly. He was good at listening and talking to people. Jim gave me some sound advice in my early days: 'If you start to hate the job, get out because it will make your life a misery.' These particular words would later mean a lot to me.

The shifts passed very quickly and it wasn't long before I was out on my own, thinking on my own two feet.

My first child was born during this time and this played a major part in changing my outlook on life. I started to realise that the horrible things I saw and witnessed in society were eventually going to affect her life one day. A thin layer of nice people seemed to cover the surface of society but I soon found that underneath was a large population of scum prepared to live like parasites off other people's misery.

On dark nights I risked life and limb arresting persistent offenders, challenging groups of men when little or no back-up was available. Lack of resources and manpower in the overstretched sections were getting far too common. I was fleet of foot and, being very fit from my career in the Corps, found other police officers' general fitness laughable.

The lists of violent confrontations soon became endless, each being quickly forgotten with the next. This in itself started to have an effect on me. I would go home having worked a 12- or 14-hour shift and somehow try and switch off and go to sleep. It was sometimes impossible but I could cope, couldn't I?

When my daughter's christening arrived I felt rather proud. She was perfect in every way. I tried to suppress the memories of the poor sick children I had seen in Iraq and Manchester. I wanted her to have the best possible start in life. By the end of the evening most of my friends and family had left the party at the house, but a few of us from work decided to go to the local pub and then return home with a takeaway to finish off what had been a memorable day. That was until Jim, another friend, Gordon, and I walked into the local Indian restaurant. Talking to Jim, I became aware of four men entering the takeaway. I paid little or no attention to them until I suddenly saw one of these blokes punch Gordon in the face for no apparent reason.

In the same instant I felt a shocking blow to my face, which caused me to fall forward over a knee-high coffee table. As I hit the floor I lost consciousness.

After a moment I was being dragged to my feet by Jim whilst one of the men hit out at me. Hot blood was in my mouth and running from my nose. Glancing down, I saw that I was covered in dark red blood that was now gushing from my nose. I could feel my face tightening as the swelling started.

I lost consciousness again, and I finally awoke in the local A&E department, where I had been admitted suffering from a severely fractured nose, two smashed front teeth and a blood clot behind my eye socket, along with a badly swollen face. The injury to my nose and teeth required a total of four operations and the perpetrators of this unprovoked attack were never found. The attack knocked my confidence a little and brought me back to reality. I now had first-hand experience of what it was like to be a victim of an unprovoked violent crime. I wasn't going to let it happen again!

Before long I was back in uniform, attending stabbings and violent incidents; alcohol usually played a major contributing role. One such incident was outside a pub where two brothers had decided to attack another youth with a knife. They inflicted a knife wound to his stomach, which had exposed his intestines, before leaving him for dead. In their drug-and-alcohol-induced state they decided to attack another man on his way home from a night out. I arrived shortly after the second attack, quickly being joined by my colleagues. Because of the confusion and drunken state of all involved, we had little choice but to arrest everyone at the scene.

The main offender was completely unreasonable, high on a concoction of drugs and drink. He required hospital treatment, having sustained deep lacerations to his fingers when he had stabbed each of his victims. It took three of us to get him processed through the busy A&E department and he seemed oblivious to what he had done. However, the two brothers were eventually convicted at Manchester Crown Court, one receiving a life sentence for attempted murder.

After a few years, because of my commitment to the job, I got involved in the divisional crime squad. This was a proactive team designed to target the local drug dealers. We had a good team of three experienced detectives and a number of seconded uniformed officers. This new challenge took me into the world of handling informants and obtaining intelligence. For my own reasons and the safety of operational officers I will not be describing this process. The informants had many reasons for helping the police but 99 per cent of the time it was for financial reward. I began to realise that although the force encouraged informant handling, it was fraught with danger and aggravation.

An informant was normally a criminal who would try anything to get himself out of trouble if arrested. On occasions this even resulted in officers being called to court when an informant was a defendant and claiming he was of good character. It was complete bollocks and far more trouble than it was worth. All sorts of accusations and allegations could be made against individual officers if they stepped across the white line of guidance set by a Home Office which had little idea about life on the streets and dealing with low-life informers.

I went on many dawn raids, executing warrants for drugs, stolen articles and firearms. Some information that came into the office required immediate action otherwise intelligence could be lost.

One particular afternoon we got a tip-off that a local man was dealing drugs from his flat. Putting a quick plan together, it was decided that an officer (Stuart) would visit the address in plain clothes and make a test purchase from the alleged dealer. He would walk to the flat whilst being tailed by an undercover welfare officer. The remainder of the team would then plot up in unmarked cars ready to react if Stuart got into difficulties.

Everything started well. Stuart's movements were outlined by the welfare officer and we waited with bated breath. The final approach left Stuart out of sight of the whole team. It was now the most demanding and dangerous part of the operation.

A few minutes later Stuart reappeared but not as expected. To our astonishment the alleged dealer was accompanying him from the flat. Everyone involved was wondering what the hell Stuart was playing at.

It went chaotic over the radio but we had to accept his reasons for walking away with the target. We were not in a position to prejudge Stuart's decision because we didn't have a clue what was happening. We had to ensure that Stuart was going to be OK, whilst remaining out of sight.

The task of remaining out of sight on a busy housing estate in Manchester where crime was rife was extremely hard. Needless to say, we lost sight of Stuart. The sergeant in charge started to earn his money. He had to call the shots but seemed to accept what Stuart was doing. He was seen going to another address, and again we waited with bated breath for him to reappear.

Contingency plans were being discussed about what to do next. Stuart's welfare had become the number one concern even if it meant blowing the job.

However, after a few more minutes Stuart appeared from around a corner in quick step. I instantly recognised by the way he was walking that he had scored some drugs. Back with us, he quickly recounted events.

To his complete surprise the target had offered to help him get some drugs from another dealer because he was out. After the short walk across the estate to the unknown address, a woman met him and sold him a bag of brown (heroin).

We needed to act fast, so we traced the target walking back to his flat and quickly arrested him. The next move was to get into the house where the woman was selling heroin. Smashing our way in through the front door with the Wam-Ram (entry tool), we recovered a substantial amount of drugs, to the dismay of the mother inside.

The real dangers that police officers are exposed to every day when gaining entry into a house quickly became apparent. Under the bed in the back bedroom was a loaded sawn-off shotgun, pistol and .22 rifle. The woman's boyfriend, who owned the guns, wasn't at the address when we entered; however, he arrived whilst we were conducting the search. He too was quickly arrested. But the outcome of the operation could have been totally different if he had been in the house when we forced our way in. We rode our luck on many occasions.

The defence the boyfriend later provided in court for being in possession of the weapons was that he had been looking for the men responsible for burgling his father's house. This didn't wash with the jury and he was later sentenced to 15 years' imprisonment.

I was enjoying the crime squad but, as had happened in the Corps, when things started to work well, a new boss would arrive and decide to change things. The turnover in management was bad to say the least, affecting everyone's performance until they knew how the new boss operated. After 12 months and some very good results, incuding the recovery of firearms and drugs, I was thrown out of plain clothes back into uniform. This was called the tenure policy, and I hated it.

With a new addition to my family, I had to get on with the job and put my concerns behind me. These included the sights and sounds I witnessed every day. The ever-increasing demands on the dropping number of officers on duty meant that we were severely stretched. Like many of the officers I worked with, I put the anxieties to the back of my mind and went on running around like a headless chicken. The GMP is busier than any other force in the country, and on occasions I didn't even get a chance to get a pen out, let alone have a drink.

Giving evidence was always nerve-racking and I soon became disheartened by the system and the way police officers and key prosecution witnesses were treated by the system. The lawyers were just making money from misery. The majority were totally out of touch with the harsh realities of life on the street, baffling juries with sometimes very irrelevant issues. (I won't be giving examples, in order to allow those involved in the criminal justice system to ponder on their own experiences.) At any opportunity they would attempt to humiliate a witness in front of a magistrate or jury.

From my experiences, it wasn't justice I was witnessing but a stage performance and all I had to do was play my part in the production. I hadn't joined for that. I yearned for something better but family and financial pressures stopped me. I realised I was a name and number again; a rubbing rag for the arrogant barristers, a piece of shit in a uniform to the defendants or somebody to blame by the disillusioned public.

Nobody cared about the individual officers, although the glossy quotes and phrases in the press and other publications tried to suggest otherwise. The police service was mentally hard and very difficult to get away from.

Any time I was introduced to somebody, it was always, 'He's a copper.' People would instantly look at me as if I was a threat to their socialising. This really annoyed me and made it difficult to meet people outside the job. The majority of my friends in the Police were genuine people, trying to earn a living and doing something worth while. Many of them soon became disillusioned by the system and I saw how people changed over the years. On entry the majority were naive and from good honest backgrounds. They would believe everything that was said to them and try to talk to people as they expected to be spoken to themselves. This may have worked for officers outside the big cities but nearly all the people I came into contact in the city environment were horrible examples of the human race. I started to lose faith in human beings. I got little respite from obnoxious, unreasonable drunken people. I had lost trust in everyone outside my close circle of friends and family because I didn't get much chance in between shifts to meet nice normal individuals.

It was stress, stress, stress – pressure from bosses who had lost touch with front-line policing or who had never spent much time on the streets before racing away with their so-called careers. Lawyers from the prosecution and defence asked stupid questions and expected officers to do their work for them. Senior officers and lawyers were very unsympathetic and unrealistic towards uniformed officers when files had ambiguities or items missing. It was all too easy for them to criticise. They weren't the ones putting the files together when adrenaline levels were coming down after potentially life-threatening situations in the middle of the night.

Eventually these factors, in conjunction with shiftwork and dealing with horrible people, had an overwhelming effect on officers' personalities. Some became obnoxious, others hated the job and moaned constantly, others dodged and left-shouldered (avoided) anything they could in order to avoid the mountains of paperwork and some, like myself, got fed up with the scrotes and the criminal justice system which we had been taught this country should be so proud of. With this came the lack of confidence, especially in those in charge. Increasingly bosses were more preoccupied by their promotion prospects and correct quotes at assessment centres than by doing the job properly.

9

A TERRIBLE CHANGE

I was now getting through another set of nights driving the divisional van. Over the preceding days my body had slowly adjusted to its nocturnal existence. Mitch had been my partner over the weekend and, with manning levels permitting, we would stay together for the remainder of the week. It was now a Sunday night in the middle of summer and, as always, Wythenshawe had seen its fair share of youths causing annoyance and fights. I was due in Crown Court in the morning and had organised with the shift sergeant to finish at 1 a.m. in order to go home and get some sleep before going to court.

Every call was always something different but I had become well practised in attending drunken disputes and domestics.

Shortly before 11 p.m. we received a call via our radio that a large group of men were fighting outside a pub in the Newall Green area of Wythenshawe. Racing to the scene, we soon got behind 'Ken' in his panda car and 'Tom', the divisional dog handler. The location was described as being close to the Freeband public house, but on arrival there didn't seem to be any sign of fighting and I started to think it might be another hoax call. Getting back in touch with the communicator, I asked him to clarify the location.

We were definitely in the right area. Mitch turned our

vehicle around and I noticed somebody making a hasty attempt to flag us down. Getting closer, he appeared frantic, waving his arms and rushing towards us.

Ken managed to stop in front of us but we quickly got out in order to speak to this person. Briefly, he told us that somebody was lying in a bush next to the road and was seriously injured.

Shining my torch into the bushes about 20 feet from the road, which was adjacent to an estate, I suddenly became aware of a man lying on the ground as if he had fallen over. As I approached him, I noticed that the grass I was walking across felt wet underfoot. Thinking this was rather odd owing to the lack of recent rain, I shone the torch at my feet.

To my horror, I immediately realised that it wasn't water but blood!

Glancing into the darkness, I saw that the victim was now trying to get up. I pushed myself into the bushes. It was a white man in his early thirties. He was conscious but seemed to be suffering from shock as he made a vain attempt to struggle to his feet. His clothing was saturated in blood, so I quickly asked him who he was and what had happened.

He replied desperately, 'My name's Robert, I'm a corporal in the Army, home on leave, and a group of kids jumped me.'

Ken and Tom were trying to find where he was bleeding. At the same time Mitch was frantically trying to put some light on us and get the first-aid kits from our vehicles.

The man called Robert began to realise the extent of his injuries and attempted to get up again. Telling him not to panic and lie down, I hastily fumbled for my radio and called for an ambulance. Still scrambling in the bushes,

Robert began crying. He was fighting hard, telling me he was going to die if we didn't get him to hospital. I had now moved my face close to his in order to hear what he was saying. His voice became quieter and I saw the life drain from his eyes as they began to dilate and roll in his head. He was becoming incoherent, but I could make out, 'Get my mum, I want my mum.'

Our eyes became fixed on one another as he slipped in and out of consciousness. I screamed at him to stay awake and not fall asleep, but I knew deep down he had lost vast amounts of blood. His pulse was very shallow and I struggled in my haste to find it. Tom and Ken had managed to remove part of his jeans in an attempt to find his main injuries. Glancing along his weakening body, I saw that he was suffering from a number of stab wounds to his legs and stomach. No blood was coming from the wounds in his stomach but his white legs were covered in clots and dark arterial blood.

Suddenly our eyes met again as I kept repeating his name in an attempt to keep him conscious. His eyes became locked on mine once more and I slowly watched him begin to die.

'Where's the fucking ambulance?' I kept saying. 'Where's the fucking ambulance?'

By now he was gripping me around the shoulders as I knelt over him. With each passing second his grip grew weaker and weaker and I felt like crying. Here I was, minutes from the nearest A&E department, and a complete stranger was about to die in my arms. And all I could do was sit there.

Other officers, including my inspector, began to arrive, so I shouted at him that we needed to move this man before he died as there was still no sign of the ambulance.

All he said to me was, 'It's your decision.'

I wasn't paid to make these kinds of decisions. That's what I had an inspector for, wasn't it?

GMP, or at least my shift, had an unspoken rule that anybody who was injured should not be conveyed in a police vehicle.

I had to make a decision for my own sake and conscience. I told the lads that we needed to move him into the van and get him to hospital ASAP. They all agreed, so we quickly picked up this large unconscious man and struggled towards our van. Whilst doing this I tried to monitor whether or not he was still breathing but I soon realised that he had stopped. Getting to the kerb, I attempted mouth to mouth but it was of little use.

Then somebody shouted that the ambulance had arrived. The paramedics seemed to know that he was in a bad way. One threw a resuscitation device and asked me if I knew how to use it.

I wanted to shout, 'Of course I fucking know how to use it! Where the fuck have you been?' But, quickly getting on with my job of resuscitation, I jumped into the back of the ambulance and watched the paramedics attempt to get venflons into his collapsed veins. But on reaching the A&E department I knew he was dead.

Getting out of the ambulance, I felt numb and in shock myself. But yet again I pushed my emotions to the back of my mind and attempted to compose myself.

As I walked into the hospital reception area to give the staff Robert's details, I was suddenly swamped by people. The group started shouting and screaming hysterically, wanting answers to countless questions. I couldn't answer them because I honestly didn't know what the hell had happened to Robert. I went into a shocked trance for a few seconds and everything around me went silent. Here I was recovering from the death of a complete stranger in my arms and all these people wanted to do was shout at me. I glanced at myself in the reflection of a drinks machine. I saw that my expressionless face hid the trauma it had just witnessed and my white shirt was covered in blood smears where the young man had gripped me until his last breath.

'I'm his mum. What's happened?' At this I snapped out of my trance.

A nurse had obviously seen the group of people congregating around me and decided to help. She led us to a relatives' room, where the parents then began asking me how their son was. I didn't really know because at that stage I somehow believed the A&E staff would bring him round. I switched into police mode and told them that their son was in a serious condition and excused myself.

I was talking on my radio and updating the control room on the situation, when the consultant walked out of the resuscitation room with Mitch behind him. 'The young man has died,' he told me. I already knew this but it was still a shock.

We decided to go straight to his mother and father and deliver the worst news anyone could ever hear.

How do you tell parents that their son has been murdered? I couldn't remember what I said but it was so, so sad. I would never want anyone to have to hear those words. By now the whole family had arrived and all I could do was comfort them. I was still in a state of shock but I couldn't show any kind of emotion because I was mentally drained.

In between this flood of grief I had a job to do. By now the investigation was rapidly snowballing. Blood samples, witnesses, evidence and many more questions that required answers were all needed.

For forensic purposes and the coroner's benefit, I had to remain at the hospital and have Robert formally identified to me by his heart-broken family.

A few moments earlier he was called 'Robert', now he was just being referred to as 'the body' in the radio transmissions.

Mentally and physically shattered, I eventually left for home at 6 a.m. Tom and Mitch were the only ones who spoke to me and asked if I was OK. I drove home in a daze, with the incident repeatedly running through my mind like a video on automatic play-back. Walking through the front door, I fell to my knees and cried. I had never felt so traumatised.

I didn't sleep and, before I knew it, I was driving to Crown Court to give evidence in an unrelated case. This was crazy. I felt that nobody gave a damn about my condition, especially the senior officers on my division. The lawyers, the judge and judicial clerks just wanted the case to be heard. I had to wait. I sat outside the court and repeatedly thought about what I had been doing only 11 hours earlier. My mind was racing and nobody I spoke to that day had any idea how stressed and traumatised I was.

I went straight back to work, and a week or so after the incident it was just another murder for the police to deal with. Management moved and changed but I was still left with my personal guilt. I couldn't get the sights and sounds of Robert out of my mind, and the lads Tom, Ken and Mitch all seemed to be coping better than me.

One afternoon a welfare officer came to the station and the four of us who had been at the scene were asked to sit around a table and discuss it. Now I know we should have had private counselling after such a traumatic event. Nobody, including myself, was going to stand up in front of the six people present and admit to being stressed and unable to think straight. At the time it wasn't the way I had been accustomed to think. It was rammed to the back of my memory filing cabinet in the hope I could just forget it.

Throwing myself back into work and desperately seeking a move, I successfully passed an interview to become a trainee detective.

My six-month traineeship was to be at Hall Lane, where I had worked on the crime squad. It was ideal because I knew the local criminals, which could only be to my advantage. Billy, my tutor detective, couldn't have been any better. He had a wealth of experience and a great ability to pass on what he knew in a very professional manner. Coupled with this, he had a great sense of humour when he wasn't moaning.

From the very first day in the CID office I dealt with a wide range of serious crime: rapes, street robberies, armed robberies, stabbings, criminal deceptions and murder. At times the pressure could quickly mount up but Billy and I got on with the job and we became good partners and friends. His humour took my mind away from the trauma of Robert's murder. The ever-present images would drift in and out of my mind but I began to use work as a tool to forget the scenes. I could go for weeks without any problem, then the slightest thing would trigger the flashbacks, leading to sleepless nights and lack of concentration. Even bumping into Ken, Mitch and Tom and not discussing the scene somehow reactivated my mind again.

The six months soon came to an end, and I had achieved the reports necessary to progress as a detective. Fortunately, I was seconded to Hall Lane CID until a full-time vacancy became available. In this time I also had to pass a six-week CID course and the relevant exams.

I continually feared going back into uniform. The bottled-up trauma, stress and anticipation of dealing with violent confrontations stirred these emotions.

Then one day when I walked into the office the civilian typist turned around to me and said, 'The DCI told me to tell you, you will be going back into uniform on Monday.'

I didn't think much of him for leaving the message with the typist. I would have paid the man far more respect if he had spoken to me in person.

Come the following Monday, I found myself donning a uniform and driving around mopping up the pieces until a vacancy in the CID became available. I was very close to quitting. It was only my family and friends that stopped me.

Off-duty I had also changed. I didn't like going out. I found it hard to relax in pubs and places where lots of people gathered. I became so conscious of who was near to me, anticipating everyone as a threat of some kind. My mind raced away with itself every time I stepped from the house. I was becoming worse but still I pushed the emotions to the back of my mind.

I was at an all-time low. Mel and I had applied to emigrate to New Zealand but to our distress we had been rejected over a disputed qualification and the lack of one point!

I went to work in a trance-like state. Finally, I received a call from my old detective inspector. He was running the CID at Greenheys Police Station in Moss Side. Nobody really wanted to work there and, being an ex-Marine officer, he asked me if I wanted to join the office. I jumped at the chance because I wanted out of uniform.

*   *   *

209

The short move from Wythenshawe to Moss Side was like moving to another world. Moss Side was the gangland area of South Manchester. Its large cosmopolitan community of Afro-Caribbeans, Africans, Asians, whites and many others was accustomed to violence and drugs.. As in the Bronx in New York, a large metal fence circled the police station. The proportion of serious crime was immense. Street robberies on the student community were rife and I'm certain not everyone reported the thefts. The numbers of shooting incidents were incredible. Lots went unnoticed by the press. Cars, taxis, pedestrians, cyclists, houses and pubs were all potential targets. In every incident we dealt with, drugs were always an underlying factor as the gangs fought for control. None of these greedy parasitic animals gave a hell for the innocent people nearby when they blasted rounds off in the street.

Nobody ever wanted to help the police, yet they blamed us for the lack of control and number of shootings. The easy option every time was to blame the police for the problems. I would visit victims of this gun culture in hospital suffering from potentially dangerous injuries, only to be met by a wall of silence. No-one who lived in the area was prepared to help, even if we could offer protection from these criminals. All the police could try and do was keep the lid on the problem, contain it and flood the area with officers, budget permitting.

My workload increased and whilst dealing with a team of street robbers, the inevitable murder occurred.

At about 10 p.m. on a November night in 1997 a 29-year-old Taiwanese student from Manchester University, Chin Yu Chang, left his home address and crossed a city centre park. Whilst walking across the park he was attacked by a group of men. His gold ring and cash were stolen from him, and he was stabbed twice. One wound penetrated his thigh and the second his chest, puncturing his heart. Left for dead by his attackers, Chang bravely staggered out of the park onto a busy road. He collapsed immediately outside the park and a number of passers by rushed to his aid. Despite attempts from the paramedics at the scene and massive transfusions of blood at the local A&E department, Chang died of his injuries the following morning.

Walking into the office later that morning, I was told to drop everything and go over to the incident room. I was now on the murder enquiry.

The superintendent who was running the case was a gentleman and a good motivator of the team. He was a methodical man who had a fantastic memory for events, facts and fiction. He had an element of the Corps about him, with his attention to detail, but not everyone on the enquiry would have agreed with me.

Some 20 officers sat in the briefing and I was thrown in at the deep end. One of the suspects had handed himself in and I was given the stressful job of conducting the interviews, along with an excellent detective sergeant.

We were both under pressure from the outset of the enquiry, and the investigation rapidly progressed as more suspects from the gang were arrested and interviewed. Come the end of the first week, all four suspects had been charged with the murder of Mr Chang.

Dealing with the evidence-gathering and interviews was perhaps the easy part of the investigation. Somebody now had to sit down and write it up. 'Rio', a DC from Greenheys, and I, were given this pleasure. Rio was brilliant. He was a good detective, with a wealth of experience and without him I would have probably found it difficult to get the job done. He was a stereotypical detective: overweight, smoked consistently and liked a drink or two. Above all he had a wicked sense of humour and I found him extremely funny and very easy to get on with.

Although I had the task of the prosecution file, the whole enquiry was a classic example of good teamwork. I developed well and learned from the experience. But underneath my professional and unemotional exterior, I was struggling mentally with the stress of the job.

The New Year saw the key suspect in the Chang case, Karl Christopher Connerton, being discharged at the magistrates' committal proceedings due to a lack of evidence. Shortly after his release he went on to commit a nasty aggravated rape at knifepoint in a woman's house.

Rio and I got extreme pleasure in arresting him for the rape, based on DNA evidence, and for Mr Chang's murder. A tape-recorded admission had been obtained by relatives of the co-accused, and this was enough additional evidence to charge him again with the murder.

Connerton was later jailed for life at Manchester Crown Court for the murder of Mr Chang. Three other defendants also received jail terms ranging from ten to fifteen years. All four of the gang were white. It was a sad time for the relatives of Mr Chang but it had given me immense professional satisfaction when the jury returned the guilty verdicts.

But the pleasure of a good court result was short-lived because the shooting, stress and responsibilities of being the night detective again overtook events. I was still mentally simmering but had little time to dwell on my problem.

The CID office at Greenheys now had a new acting detective inspector from our neighbouring police station,

Longsight. Rumours were rife, and they seemed glad to see the back of him. He treated everyone with contempt and appeared to think officers were always trying to bullshit him. As expected, morale soon dived in the office. I spoke to him only when I had to.

During a large investigation I had been tasked with tracing a workman in Moss Side who had witnessed two police officers being threatened with a Mach 10 machine pistol. The weapon was not fired but this was more luck than the defendant's lack of trying, as it jammed in some way.

Being a committed DC and the fact it was colleagues and an ex-Marine who had been threatened, I did my utmost to win the confidence of the crucial witness. He had nothing to do with the incident but offered his public-spirited commitment to attend court and give his evidence, although he was scared because of the violent background of the defendant and his associates.

The night before the trial, the witness contacted me and explained he was having transport difficulties. I had to get authority either to collect him myself or get another DC to do the job. Overtime constraints were a problem so I automatically approached the DI. Greater Manchester Police had assured the public that it was committed to helping witnesses when attending court, but the words from my DI couldn't have been further from that aim.

'Tell him to get the train and make his own way to court. If he doesn't turn up, the court will issue a warrant. I'm not sending anyone to get him.'

My jaw dropped open and the DS present could sense my frustration as I gazed at the DI in total amazement. I had a genuine witness who had nothing to gain from attending court in a city he didn't even live in. He was doing his bit, but I had to tell him to get his own arse to court because my boss didn't give a shit. The DI certainly lived up to his reputation and I began to loathe him.

I was getting tired of the constraints, overtime, lack of morale, lack of resources and above all no let-up. I cannot speak for the other officers at Greenheys but the atmosphere was far from happy. Management meetings would come up with all sorts of daft ideas. They would spend hours listening to suggestions and concerns but nothing ever changed, mainly because there was no money. After one particular meeting the DI came out with this comment: 'Please ensure you sign the journal [message book] and underline it!'

Here I was working in one of the most violent places in the country, where teenagers ran around carrying weapons more commonly found on battlefields, and all the management could say was underline the journal!

Management was very poor at times. Some senior police officers thought they had good business aptitude. They held overtime money back until the end of the financial year and would then lash out on worthless operations to use the budget up and prevent its loss the following financial year.

From a practical point of view this method of management hindered the day-to-day work of operational officers. Cases would be lost at court because officers had to hand over investigations at the end of a shift as there was allegedly no overtime. 'Too many cooks spoil the broth', and in complex investigations specific facts could be misinterpreted or even lost.

Witness intimidation was all too apparent in the violent streets of Manchester and the Police Service was losing its ability to protect the people. In a violent society those who helped the cops were easy targets. The courts seemed to be unaware of, or chose to ignore, the people willing to help the out-of-date criminal justice system. In my opinion, solicitors, jurors and the judges themselves will soon become targets for the criminals of this country. The culture of drugs, violence and money-making is a problem that needs to be addressed quickly as it is a form of cancer that is slowly spreading into the depths of everyone's life. Everyone I came into contact with in my line of duty seemed to be demoralised with the system, although most would not openly admit this.

I was slowly losing all my motivation. I was still suffering underneath and decided I could try to rectify this by a transfer to another force and get away from the city. I chose Cambridgeshire.

Work in the meantime continued. One afternoon I was writing away when I made the fatal error of picking up the phone. The police communicator informed me that a man had called the 999 system and said he had stabbed his friend two days ago and was wondering if we had found him, and confirmed he would meet officers at a church in Altrincham at 7.30 p.m.

I went to the stabbed man's address with my DS Alison and partner DC Rob.

Alison was a good experienced detective sergeant from the old school of thought. I enjoyed working with her because although she was still theoretically my boss, she was willing to listen to our comments on everything. Sometimes she agreed but was always diplomatic when she didn't.

Rob had recently returned to the CID office at Greenheys after an attachment at NCIS (National Criminal Intelligence Service) in London. He was still trying to adjust to the fast pace of life in the office but instantly became a good friend. He gave the impression that he was fine, but underneath he was finding it hard to get over his marriage break-up, coupled with the fact that he too seemed disillusioned by the jobs we had to do. Alison and Rob both had a good sense of humour, which help me considerably when times got stressful.

Arriving at the address, I discovered it was a large Victorian house which had been converted into squalid flats. The flat in question was located on the top floor and our initial enquiries of the other tenants revealed that no-one had seen the occupant of the flat.

We obtained the keys from the landlord, and I cautiously opened the door, whilst everyone stood behind me. Slowly I pushed the door ajar, immediately noticing a distinct musty smell and the sound of a radio playing in the background. Adrenaline started flowing through my body, which increased my heart rate. The palms of my hands started perspiring as the flight or fight factor kicked in and prepared me for action. Glancing into the flat, I was met by the sight of a man lying face down on a carpet in the centre of the room. Protruding from the base of his skull was a red-handled kitchen knife.

It didn't take me long to see that the man was dead and had been for sometime. The T-shirt he wore exposed his arms, which were now mottled blue and pink. The sides of his face were a darker shade of blue verging on purple. Carefully looking around to check nobody else was in the flat, I retraced my steps and left.

Once I had shut the door, the hectic events at the beginning of a murder inquiry ensued, when hours feel like minutes and the mind is abuzz with information. I was the exhibits officer, with responsibilities to record all the items seized as evidence and to accompany the body to the local mortuary once the forensic evidence had been obtained.

Lifting the lifeless body into a body bag, I made my way with the undertakers to identify the body to the mortician.

Having had little sleep, I was back at work the following morning documenting exhibits. A man was in custody and I had a post mortem (PM) to attend. These were far from pleasant and I tried not to think of what I was looking at. During the PM I documented every item handed to me by the pathologist as the hours ticked by. When I had finished this grim work, I cleaned up, grabbed my bag of exhibits and walked out of the mortuary onto the main road into Manchester. Then I stopped in my tracks. I was coming out of a barbaric scene to life passing me by. People were going about their business totally unaware of the sights that had been happening 50 feet away inside the mortuary. I was close to the edge of normality as I held my bag of body bits.

Whilst investigating serious violence and murder, I realised the fine line between life and death. The carnage normally resulted from very trivial matters. The man I found with the kitchen knife in his head had died as a result of an argument over the sale of a weights bench. In another case a young man had a chisel forced into his skull during an altercation over a girl on the way home from a pub. It was all very pitiful and all I could do was bottle up my thoughts about these pathetic individuals who committed these crimes. I certainly had no sympathy for them or their barbaric acts.

I didn't realise it but these sights were slowly chipping away at my sanity. I thought I was OK and able to cope with the trauma. Deep down, I believed a move to a new force was the answer. I was wrong! Nobody from my force knew the real reasons I was leaving because I didn't. I used excuses of why I was transferring to hide my fear of being seen as a failure.

Packing, interviews, new schools and planning dates for

the sale of my house were all preoccupying my mind as I attempted to leave the memories behind me in Manchester by moving to Cambridgeshire. I wasn't sad about leaving GMP. I was getting used to changes and meeting new people. But every time I started settling down, the memories and horrific scenes would start to reappear.

I now know that I was running away from my fears and stress. A few days before leaving Greenheys somebody in the office handed me an article from a police magazine about post-traumatic stress disorder. Reading it I started to see myself being described. In an attempt to convince myself that I wasn't traumatised and perfectly all right, I folded the article up and put it in my wallet.

The move to Cambridgeshire was great. Mel and the children settled quickly into our new lifestyle. I initially felt better and happy in the peaceful and less intimidating atmosphere of a village.

That was until I started drawing my uniform again at the police headquarters in Huntingdon. As I sat calmly waiting to be measured into my uniform, my mind began racing back over the scenes of horror. In the mirror I saw a completely different person. I was starting to hyperventilate and sweating uncontrollably as the adrenaline levels started kicking in. I didn't understand what was happening, but I felt confused and very frightened.

Starting at the new police station in a different force was frenetic to say the least. I felt as if I was being treated like a raw recruit and began to despise the system again. The police officers were different in that they looked less stressed owing to the lack of crime. Many appeared rather immature but happy with the work they did. Most of them aspired to be traffic officers, which I found hard to accept. I didn't want to summons people for minor traffic offences or give out speeding tickets to decent hard-working people. I had jumped from an environment where violence was some how socially accepted to one where trivial matters became unduly important.

Nobody gave a damn about me; I was another name and number on the duty sheet. Every time I drove to work I started to feel angry and anxious about the tour of duty and what lay ahead. But policing in the small Cambridgeshire town was at the other end of the scale from what I had grown used to: little crime, officers who had plenty more time to conduct their enquiries and a noticeable gap between the CID and uniform officers. The social standing of officers appeared to be much higher and people actually wanted to help the police with enquiries. Every time I stopped a vehicle I expected to be faced with abuse and a potentially hostile confrontation, but it was completely opposite. The people I came into contact with seemed more courteous and willing to listen.

I was in a state of shock and because of this extra time on my mind I thought more and more about my past. The flashbacks began to start again, slowly increasing. Everything I came into contact with triggered the flashbacks, no matter how trivial, from football stars with short hair on TV to using a knife in the kitchen. I felt I was going mad, and I started having difficulty sleeping again.

Eventually it came to a head when I discovered a man breaking into a shop in the middle of the night. Chasing this local drug addict, I pursued him alone on foot into a dark, disused garage. He held an iron bar ripped from the shop shutter and I stood facing his silhouette with a small can of CS spray. Thankfully he decided to come out without a fight. My mind and adrenaline went into overdrive. My lips and limbs trembled as I fought hard to control myself in front of my colleagues. Getting to the station, I found it hard to concentrate and my memory went blank.

The procedure in the charge office amazed me. Here I was with a potentially violent man whom I had handcuffed for my own safety, but the new breed of custody sergeant didn't even look at me and spoke to the prisoner in parrot-fashion.

'How are you? Have you got any complaints against this officer? Please let me see the handcuffs. Are they on too tight?'

What a load of bollocks! The sergeant was more interested in the welfare of a shit bag-burglar than me. For fuck sake, he was supposed to be *my* sergeant.

This incident, common enough for any police officer, turned out to be my final straw. I had visited the well of courage a final time to discover it had run dry. I wasn't prepared to do it any more. Sitting at the parade room table trying to relive the event and write my statement, I kept thinking how lucky I was. It could so easily have turned the other way, as I had seen so many times in the city. Closing my eyes to concentrate on my statement, I kept seeing a body on a metal table during a post mortem with my face on it. I was mentally exhausted and had to leave this job before I got any sicker. How could I do it?

Over the years I had slowly developed the classic signs and symptoms of post-traumatic stress disorder (PTSD). I had heightened awareness of everything around me, thinking something was going to happen all the time. This was particularly relevant when out shopping in close confines with other people. I felt very uncomfortable around large groups of people and didn't like going out unless it was just to a quiet local pub with close friends. If I did manage to be persuaded to go out, I would get drunk to calm my fears and anxiousness. I had problems sleeping, nightmares and hot flushes. I began avoiding activities such as team sports, making all kinds of excuses not to meet people. I lost all feelings and sympathy towards others and at times felt detached from colleagues at work. I would get angry over the minor obstacles and found it difficult to concentrate.

Finally, after another sleepless night, I decided to seek help and use the confidential counselling service offered by Cambridgeshire Police. The decision wasn't straightforward and I paced around my house wondering about it. The effort required to make the call was one of the toughest I have ever had to make. I walked to the phone, dialled three numbers, put it down, then paced around again, dialled the number and put the phone down again. Eventually I managed it, and a female voice answered.

A surge of emotion leapt from me and I broke down and fell to my knees. I tried to speak, but nothing came out as I sobbed and sobbed. A traumatic pressure valve holding back years of restrained emotions had been released. After a good ten minutes without being able to speak I started to talk to the very understanding lady. I talked about my memories and found it easy to confide in this complete stranger.

The result of this call sent me on the long road to recovery, which saw me leaving the Police.

The years had passed quickly, and I was the last person to think I would suffer from such a silent illness when I set out for Lympstone so long ago.

I feel very bitter and angry towards the Police for their

lack of concern. Nobody ever asked me how I was or if I was OK when I left Manchester. Like so many retired police officers, I thought hard about taking my plight down the compensation avenue. But although financially this could have compensated me, I didn't wish to put my family through the legal circus.

My time in Cambridgeshire had been a total of six months. They had inherited my illness but fortunately had a confidential system that helped me, and I thank their force doctor.

I wanted to write this book solely about the Marines but I felt the need to tell my story to its conclusion. Undoubtedly there will be many more victims who will suffer from this illness; nobody ever knows their limits until they actually reach them.

As for me, I have tried to move on with my life after some lengthy therapy. Treatment has not cured me totally as the intrusive memories and flashbacks continue. Mentally I have learned to control them better and put them into some sort of context within my life. Physically I am still very fit, and the writing and planning of this book has helped me overcome my fear over the years.

Fortunately, I was able to find work within a family business whilst I put my life back on track. But undoubtedly the main source of my recovery has been my wife Mel, who has supported me so well over the years, putting herself and a career in nursing aside because of my inability to settle. The sleepless nights and my rash behaviour and irritability over trivial matters tested her to the limits. The dedication she has given to the children and me is something that I will always be in her debt for and I love her so much for it.

* * *

Looking back over my time in the Police, I find it nice to think of all the great people I have worked with. It is impossible to name them all but they will know who they are. I have read many books about armed actions and military stories, some true and some allegedly true. This is probably a less gung-ho account of one such life. I have tried to introduce things as I have sensed and seen them, to show what living life in the fast lane of excitement did to me.

Life is too short to miss out on the exciting things, so I can only encourage people to do what they want, but in turn be prepared to deal with the mental backlash if this invisible injury strikes.